Leaving the Shoreline

Leaving the Shoreline

A survival guide for the new manager

DR. GRANT ARMSTRONG

INSOMNIAC PRESS

Library and Archives Canada Cataloguing in Publication

Armstrong, Grant, 1954-, author
Leaving the shoreline / Grant Armstrong.

Issued in print and electronic formats.
ISBN 978-1-55483-217-0 (softcover).--ISBN 978-1-55483-221-7 (PDF)

1. Management. 2. Leadership. 3. Supervision. 4. Executives.
I. Title.

| HD31.2.A76 2018 | 658 | C2018-905793-9 |
| | | C2018-905794-7 |

Printed and bound in Canada
Insomniac Press
520 Princess Avenue, London, Ontario, Canada, N6B 2B8
www.insomniacpress.com

To Caren

Contents

Preface

My leadership journey started forty-two years ago when I left high school—or rather was asked to leave in an abrupt disagreement that amounted to a conflict of ideological stances in the pursuit of education. My English teacher thought I should attend classes; I disagreed. At that point, I entertained the idea of playing professional hockey or possibly joining the Beach Boys. Neither idea panned out. Shortly after returning from a short sabbatical in Daytona Beach, I received a call from a good friend of mine who was working at a local dairy plant. He asked if I was interested in a job. I reluctantly agreed to give it a try, and after a few days of piling crates of milk in a warehouse, I was offered a full-time job.

It's important to understand that the industrial sector was still in full force in 1975, and there were more jobs than workers, so it wasn't that they wanted me in particular; they simply wanted a warm body that could work in a warehouse, and there I was. When I started out, I had no aspirations of advancing in my career. Hell, I didn't even feel I had or wanted a career. I was just marking time until my big break came along, although I will admit I had no idea what that big break might be or what it might lead to.

I was offered my first supervisor role about three

years into my newfound vocation, supervising fifteen men working in the warehouse and shipping platform. Someone had seen something in me that I didn't. In most organizations back then (and, I believe, in most organizations now), a new management position was more likely to be granted to, or imposed upon, a person who had some or all of the following qualities:

- Is the best worker
- Has some administrative ability
- Seems to get along with people
- Doesn't piss the boss off too often

They are then cast into the workplace with very little or no guidance in how to manage let alone lead people. Such was and still is the life of the new manager. I was more fortunate than many new managers in that I did receive a fair amount of guidance from my boss at the time, but this was informal advice rather than structured manager development. Regardless, I ended up learning many things about management and leadership by trial, error, and sometimes disaster. This is why I decided to put together this guidebook for new managers.

I hope this book will help soften the blow of any new responsibilities you take on as a new manager. It will provide you with insights on what to expect and important tips on how to prepare yourself. My many years of experience in human resources and as a business coach have led me to understand the great disservice we do to new managers by failing to provide adequate training and preparation for one of the most critical roles in any organization: the role of the frontline manager.

In my own personal development, I eventually decided that I would be limited in my ability to advance in a larger corporation without some formal education, so I pursued and completed undergraduate, graduate, and doctoral studies with majors in business, labour studies, and education. However, the most valuable knowledge related to managing and leading people must be learned in the workplace. This book will help you by pointing out many of the nuances and applications they don't teach about at post-secondary institutions. Once you're done reading it and you find yourself working with the material, you will be well on your way to becoming the best manager you can be.

Introduction

You may wonder why I choose a nautical theme for this book. Is it because I am a sailor? No. My experience on the open water is based primarily on my very limited exposure as the owner of a canoe and eventually a Snark, a 13-foot sailboat with a maximum weight capacity of 350 pounds. I purchased the Snark in Muskoka one summer just as we were heading home to St. Catharines. We unloaded it off the trailer into our yard, and there it sat in dry dock for three years. I eventually decided to sell it rather than plant flowers in it, and so ended my sailing saga.

My decision to use a nautical theme was more based on the lure I have always felt for the ocean—its immense power and uncertainty. One day it can be calm and serene, and the next day dangerous and unyielding. Great sailors know how to read the weather, the sky, and the tides as they navigate their way through the waters. In a way, that's like experienced managers who know how to read people, opportunities, and a changing work environment. When people think about becoming a manager, they seldom consider the ever-changing waters ahead. Many fail to chart a destination before embarking on their journey or even map things out as they go.

If you're a manager already, this will probably

make sense to you—if not, imagine becoming a manager for the first time. As you sail away from the shoreline toward new responsibilities, you leave your status as an individual contributor behind. Your tack has changed. The word *tack* doesn't refer only to the position of a boat relative to the trim of its sails; it's also a term that refers to our taking a certain approach or course of action, especially when we have a specific goal in mind. In your case, you are now responsible for the actions of others; you must coordinate those actions and adjust your approaches to attain new goals. With very little formal preparation, you venture out into the sea of management and hope for smooth sailing. Instead, you encounter rough waters, rolling fog, and multidirectional winds that challenge you to chart a course to safe harbour with very little help.

This book will help you, as a new manager, balance the personal, professional, and organizational goals that propel you forward. You will learn to become aware of the various forces that influence each of these realms, including

- your attributes and skills,
- the attributes and skills of others,
- your perceptions of others,
- your professional relationships,
- your influence over others,
- how your actions affect others, and
- what you can control in your life (your career, perceptions, attributes, relationships, etc.).

From the crow's nest, you can look out and see these elements with greater clarity. As you become aware of these forces and how they work together, you will be better able to navigate them and chart a course that allows you to achieve your personal, professional, and organizational goals. Although the elements presented in this book are common to many North American managers, there is no formula for the proper tack. Each manager defines his or her goals and successes differently, but everyone can use the information presented in these pages to chart his or her own course. If you are one of the following, you will benefit from reading this book:

1. A new or emerging manager (looking for a pragmatic handbook to help transition from an individual contributor to an employee supervisor or manager)
2. An existing manager (experiencing productivity or employee relations issues or involved in the development of new managers)
3. A human resources professional (responsible for training and development, and recruitment and retention)

How to Read This Book

This not a typical management how-to book, so you won't find things in here about traditional communication techniques, time management skills, or guidelines for running effective meetings. This book focuses on the real stuff that new managers experience and can gain some control over as they chart their course. It's the kind of book you can complete in its entirety during a three-hour flight. Each chapter stands on its own merit, so you could read them in any order and still benefit greatly. However, I do suggest reading the sections in sequence because you will gain additional benefit by building on each one as you move through the book.

Each section presents a broad concept that is broken down into smaller pieces in each chapter. These include real-life stories, essential notes, and a selected set of basic rules. You will also find questions throughout the book. This is the coach in me always looking for opportunities for self-reflection and education.

Section 1 – Preparing for the Voyage: Understanding Yourself and Your Role

This section explores the move from individual contributor to manager. It will help you understand your attributes and skills as well as those of others. It will also help you put your new position in context, helping you understand the difference between management and leadership. This section also gets you started on the planning process. It includes determining what you want to achieve as well as planning the first two weeks and the first three months, which are critical time frames for the new manager.

Section 2 – Leaving Port: Casting Off the Lines and Heading Out to Sea

It is now time to cast off the lines and head out to sea away from the comfort and security of a safe harbour. Building upon what you learned in Section 1, this section delves into your influence and interactions. It also explores the most crucial of all managerial skills: communication and having "the honest conversation." Employee engagement, trust, role clarity, and leadership style are also discussed.

Section 3 – Out at Sea: The Wind in Your Sails

In Section 3, you are finally out at sea and find yourself alone on the bridge. This is often when managers begin to hear the voice of doubt. This section looks at the bigger picture and how you can navigate the shifting tides of leadership. Here you will realize you're not alone after all, and we will discuss the importance of delegation, decision-making, and developing staff.

Section 4 – Back in the Harbour: A Safe Port

The final section focuses on arriving at a safe destination. It's a time for self-reflection. You will think about what you learned, what areas you need to develop for your next voyage, and the steps you will need to take before you set sail again. This section concludes with some final considerations about leadership.

This handbook is your lighthouse built on my solid foundation of forty-two years of research and experience with managers in various organizations. It will help you find success as a manager sooner than if you simply tried to find your way on your own. You will better understand yourself and others, make confident decisions, and build positive relationships. You will become aware of the things you can control (e.g., your skills, how you treat others, the work you assign, how you communicate, the quality of work you produce, etc.) and will learn how to navigate the factors that define managerial success. Ultimately, you will prepare yourself to achieve your personal, professional, and organizational goals. You might also avoid some of the mistakes that managers make in the early stages of their careers. You will at least become aware of the impending dangers before they become serious problems. Note: Handbooks are convenient reference books with concise information about a specific topic. Fair warning: This book will not solve the world's problems, but it will help you become a more successful manager.

If you're ready for a different tack, read on.

Preparing for the Voyage: Understanding Yourself and Your Role

As I mentioned in the Preface, I once owned a Snark, a 13-foot sailboat you sit *on* more than *in*. It's pretty simple to operate, and I suspect it's a great way for any aspiring sailor to get their first experience of being propelled by the wind. Although it's a small vessel, there are certainly some challenges in helming it; you have to follow the same navigational rules and principles as any sailor would. However, it's certainly not as complicated as larger, more complex vessels. Snarks are better suited to small inland waterways as opposed to vast open bodies of water. In many ways, when a person begins their new career as a manager, it's like they're starting out in a Snark. Their department is probably small, meaning many of the issues that will arise should be fairly routine. Also, the parameters of their authority will probably be somewhat limited in the early stages.

Maybe you experienced this as a new manager. It's Monday morning. You're eating breakfast at your kitchen table. You've finished scrolling through your smartphone for emails, texts, and news. You start to imagine your first day as a manager, but you're left with more questions than answers.

"What have I gotten myself into?"

"What style of leadership will I use?"

"What will people think of me as a leader?"

"What if I can't manage all of these relationships and responsibilities?"

"What if someone figures out I'm not very good at managing people?"

With increasing anxiety, you realize you haven't really thought about who you are as a leader. You have only forty-five minutes to get to work. The good news is there is lots of time. Management isn't a single destination; it's a long journey with calm seas and precarious storms in between numerous ports of call and points of interest that will give you many chances to define and redefine who you are as a leader.

In this first section, you will learn to see this bigger picture. You will become better acquainted with the tactical side of management, including the elements within your control that you can work with to develop yourself and propel yourself toward various goals. You will start to explore what will change as you start your new role. You will learn who you are as a leader and will identify some of the winds and currents up ahead that may slow your progress.

Chapter 1

Understanding the Current: The Difference between Management and Leadership

Leadership is the single most important element in the success or failure of any organization.

I came up with this idea years ago and have used it to introduce every leadership course and lecture I've presented over the past fifteen years. When I share it, I usually see heads nodding in agreement, but every once in a while I catch the attention of someone in the audience who argues that the employees or the customers are more important to success. I love such discussions, but I always suggest that neither the customers nor the employees (including managers) would be around very long if an organization lacked good leadership. After some discussion, people start to see my point: Great products, services, and marketing campaigns will attract customers, but the long-term sustainability of an organization's success is largely dependent on its leadership.

I often hear people ask what the difference is between management and leadership. This question has been debated for some time, and there are many differing opinions. For the purposes of this book, the basic assumption I will make is that management is a position and leadership is a choice. Simply put, when you're promoted, management skills (hard skills) become your technical foundation, and this includes such things as scheduling, planning, and performance management. Leadership skills (soft skills), on the other hand, include your ability to influence, engage, and inspire people. You will need to use many different skills and attributes as a manager. The choices you make will affect others. Consequently, they will also affect your success and the success of your organization.

I have come to believe that there can be good or bad management but that there is no such thing as bad leadership. You're either a leader or you're not. There may be varying degrees between a good leader and a great leader, but "bad leadership" really amounts to a lack of leadership, so such a thing doesn't exist. When looking at people over the years who have been referred to as bad or evil leaders, we conclude that they weren't leaders in the true sense. No, these were dictators who manipulated or coerced people to get them to do their bidding. This is not leadership in the context of this book. Leadership is about moving people toward a certain goal or objective through trust, respect, influence, credibility, and support for the person and the organization.

In this section, you will learn about some of the past and current thinking about management and leadership. This will help get you thinking about yourself as a new manager, including how you lead now and how you want to lead in the future. Before getting started in your new management role, you may want to survey the current landscape of organizational behaviour and theory to understand the importance of leadership and management. Understanding the details (and the differences) will guide you and those you work with in a more positive direction.

Management

Welcome to Monday morning! You have been promoted to a management position. Now what? What does that mean? Do you have your sea legs yet? Typically, management entails having people report to you and being responsible for the duties related to a position of power. For example, as a manager, you might be responsible for the following tasks:

1. Hiring
2. Scheduling
3. Training and development
4. Short- and medium-term planning
5. Producing products or services through people
6. Terminating employment (for those not performing to standards)

There are often additional requirements, but these are generally considered core managerial tasks. Maybe you were promoted to your new position because you demonstrated some competency in these areas. If that's the case, way to go. Someone recognized in you the attributes required for managing and leading people! However, it's important to understand the key distinctions between managing and leading. As US Navy rear admiral Grace Hopper said, "No one ever managed men into battle."

Think about the military and managing new recruits, who go through basic training, routines, marching, and learning the basics of warfare before moving to battle conditions where people lose their lives. Leadership is important where soldiers put their lives at risk. Now think about a business application: the early stages of learning a job, doing the routine tasks, and understanding how to meet certain standards before moving to a critical project where people may lose their jobs if things go wrong. I don't want to suggest that we can compare the implications of going to war to doing business, but in both applications, leadership is crucial when there is a lot on the line.

In his book *Industrial and General Administration*, French mining engineer and executive Henri Fayol developed what he called the fourteen principles of management. He also created the six functions of management, which have stood the test of time. These include the following:

1. Forecasting
2. Planning
3. Organizing

4. Commanding
5. Coordinating
6. Controlling

These functions provide a great foundation for management, and over the past thirty years I have adapted some of Fayol's work into what I believe is a more current set of functions, which I refer to as technical management competencies. These include the following:

1. Accountability
2. Planning
3. Organizing
4. Controlling
5. Decision-making
6. Performance management
7. Role clarity/support
8. Financial acumen

Each of these competencies is described below.

Technical Management Competencies

1. *Accountability*. "Who's accountable for this?" I've asked this question many times, and I've lost track of how often everybody in the room simply stared at the floor (especially in the public sector). The fear that this question strikes in people is shocking. The fear of failure is over-

whelming, and it seems to overshadow any sense people might have about being successful in what they do. It always surprised me whenever people were promoted to a managerial position despite consistently avoiding being accountable for anything.

Good managers accept accountability. If something doesn't work out, they don't blame others. When the team is successful, they share the glory. Accountability takes courage. It's about being responsible for getting things done. Simply put, if someone walks into your workplace and asks who is in charge, you say, "I am."

2. *Planning*. Planning means looking forward. At any time, a new frontline manager could be looking at the next hour, day, week, month, or even year, whether planning for employee vacation time, new products, weather disruptions, labour shutdowns, maternity leaves, the ever-changing internal and external environments, etc. It's about taking into consideration all the things that could or will happen that can affect the successful operation of your department. You can't anticipate everything, but you can plan for anything you consider a relative certainty.

A colleague of mine once told me how his father served in the military and had been schooled in the six *P*s: "Proper Planning Prevents Piss-Poor Performance." In the armed forces, poor planning can cost lives. In business, poor planning can cost lost revenue or even lost jobs. Planning is about putting together a decisive set of actions to deal with changes. It's about getting ahead of problems before they occur and reducing the risk of a negative impact on the organization.

3. *Organizing*. Once the planning is done, you need to organize. This requires lining up the necessary resources, which can include systems and processes, human resources, and other operating resources. You must also consider timing, cost, and impact. Organizing is a fluid process. You will often need to organize and reorganize based on changing environments and conditions.

4. *Controlling*. As a manager, you must use the resources provided to you with the best interests of the organization in mind. This can include measuring and controlling inputs and outputs, overtime, quality, efficiency and effectiveness, and performance, including the adherence to relevant legislation and regulations.

5. *Decision-making*. This is one of the key competencies of a manager. The biggest complaint

I hear about managers is that they don't make decisions, they don't make decisions fast enough, or they make them too fast without thinking about the implications. When it comes to making important decisions, it's important to strike a balance and then provide feedback to employees who were involved in the decision-making process.

6. *Performance management.* This is management competency has become more prominent over the past twenty years, and I still don't think we do it very well. It's about setting expectations for employees and then holding them accountable for their successes and failures. It's about letting them know where they stand on an ongoing basis rather than holding their first performance discussion with them five minutes before you terminate them.

   Managers often have a tough time with these conversations, regardless of whether they're good or bad. The common excuse is that there just isn't enough time in the day, as everyone's too busy trying to get things done in the day-to-day operation of the business. However, employees tend to contribute more when they know their level of performance. If their performance is substandard, you can put plans into place to help them improve. If that doesn't work, performance discussions and any relevant documentation will help you form the case for helping employees find their true calling—in other words, employment somewhere else.

7. *Role clarity/support.* Employees are paid to do a job. We assume they know what their jobs are, but good managers make sure they know and make sure they have the support they need to do it. This seems simple enough, but I've run into many employees expressing concern and confusion about their role. This is partly due to the ever-changing world that businesses operate in. Jobs change, priorities change, and required skillsets even change occasionally. These changes are not often communicated and/or prioritized well enough in the scope of an employee's duties. Job descriptions are often years out of date, and many employees are not adequately compensated for new and/or more complex roles. Managers need to take the time to explain what the job is and what aspects have higher priorities over others.

8. *Financial acumen.* All organizations operate on some level to make money, raise money, spend money, etc. You know where I'm going with this. At the very least, managers need to understand budgets and the impact that waste, personnel, product development, etc., has on revenue and expenses. Many organizations

don't take the time to educate managers on this, so it's up to individual managers to understand how the finances of an organization work even on rudimentary level. After all, everything can't be left up to the accountants.

Behavioural Leadership

In addition to technical management competencies, I have developed a list of behavioural leadership competencies and survival competencies. Behavioural leadership competencies inform and guide management competencies, which in turn allows managers to complete management tasks effectively and efficiently while also making them good leaders. In summary, they include inspiring and developing people, coaching for performance, creating a vision, influencing others, collaborating to build engagement, and having the honest conversation. Figure 1 below defines the three very distinct but essential aspects of being a great manager. Doing only one of these doesn't necessarily mean you won't be able to do the job, but it probably means you won't be at the top of your game, or rather the game your boss will be expecting you to be in over the long term. For a new manager, the elements in the first circle are critical and are likely the reason you have been put in a management position. You might already be using some of the elements in the second circle, but many of us continue to develop and refine these throughout our career.

As you can see in the diagram, management and leadership are relational. There is a lot of overlap of skills and traits. However, managers don't lead in a vacuum of authority. To maximize the potential of your managerial position, you should lead with intention and make choices that respect your level of influence and the effect you have on relationships within the organization. The elements in the third circle are what you do to build and develop your own career in this ever-changing world.

Libraries could be filled with the number of books written about managerial topics, including the basic skills new managers need. A quick search through Amazon will reveal thousands of books about running meetings, planning, hiring and firing, and scheduling employees. This is why I won't spend a lot of time discussing these areas of management and their associated skills. Instead, I will address the areas of leadership that are less technical and more behavioural—the aspects of management they don't teach you in business school or leadership courses.

Although it might seem like you don't exert a great deal of power as a new manager, your position is inherently powerful. You have the power to make choices that draw upon your positive attributes and those of others. You can control how you respond to diverse situations. Your choices influence your style of management and leadership and your related success. Learn to identify and understand your attributes and skills, as well as those of the people you work with, so you can navigate the priorities, objectives, goals, and relationships you will work with as a manager.

Fig. 1

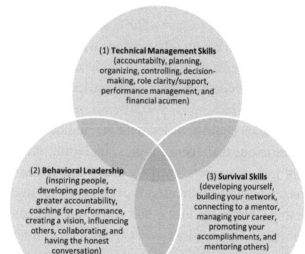

(1) **Technical Management Skills**
(accountabilty, planning,
organizing, controlling, decision-
making, role clarity/support,
performance management, and
financial acumen)

(2) **Behavioral Leadership**
(inspiring people,
developing people for
greater accountability,
coaching for performance,
creating a vision, influencing
others, collaborating, and
having the honest
conversation)

(3) **Survival Skills**
(developing yourself,
building your network,
connecting to a mentor,
managing your career,
promoting your
accomplishments, and
mentoring others)

Act Like a Leader

You will never be a leader until you believe you're a leader. This is one of the most important lessons I will have the opportunity to pass along to you. *Believing* you're a leader evolves into *acting* like a leader, and this leads to *being* a leader.

What does it mean to act like a leader? You can read volumes on this topic, including titles by noted leaders such as Jack Welch, Tom Peters, Mother Teresa, Sheryl Sandberg, and Steve Jobs. There are many stories about how these people demonstrated their greatest leadership qualities. Although you might not ever reach the same level of leadership sainthood (or, as in Mother Teresa's case, *literal* sainthood), you will demonstrate many of the same leadership qualities and achievements as you navigate your own leadership journey.

To be a leader, you need to be able to mobilize people towards a common goal. You will also need to consider relationships so you'll cause the least amount of pain and hardship to those around you. Regardless of your level of positional authority, you won't maintain trust or engagement if you fail to follow a guiding principle of respect and integrity.

At one of the businesses where I worked, the plant was located beside a retail outlet where a great deal of debris would blow around and get trapped against the fences. The janitors did a pretty good job keeping the property clean, but I noticed the plant's general manager taking matters into his own hands. He arrived early each morning and would walk along the fence and pick up garbage before going to his office.

Finally, one morning, out of guilt, I joined him. I reminded him that the janitors were available to pick up the garbage, but he explained that if each employee picked up two pieces of debris on their way from their car to the shop each morning and while returning to their car each evening, the janitors wouldn't have to spend so much time doing it and could focus their full attention on the inside areas of the workplace. I asked him if we should send out an employee email to suggest this to everyone. He didn't want to do that. He preferred to continue collecting garbage himself to set the example for others. He hoped that people would follow his lead and start to treat the plant like they did their own home. Interestingly, employees did start picking garbage up on their way in and out of the building.

This is an example of leading the way by demonstrating the behaviours you want others to copy. It also shows that even bosses can get their hands dirty. My point here is that good leaders set examples; they don't ask people to do things they wouldn't do themselves. They aren't afraid to do something that's perceived as below their station. Acting like a leader means doing things to invoke the desire in people to follow you. If you can tap into such desire even on a small level, you're more likely to achieve personal, professional, and organizational success.

Despite everything, motivating certain people can be a difficult task. Not everyone is passionate about their job. Recent studies show that only about 30 percent of employees are fully engaged in their work. The reality is that many jobs can be quite repetitive and boring, and many employees care more about their pay than they do their effort or its consequences. This means you might never be able to engage all of your workers. But if you take an active interest in people and demonstrate respect, you'll have an easier time cultivating trusting and engaged relationships with more employees.

If you're truly lucky, you will have the opportunity to work for at least one great leader in your life. Many people never get the opportunity. I've worked for two outstanding, honest, humble, and fearless leaders. Some of the stories in this book are their stories. I believe that much of their success was based on the fact that they thought of themselves as leaders. They believed wholeheartedly that they had tremendous responsibility for their organization and, more important, for their employees. In some cases, this even extended into their community.

Survival Skills

I have separated survival skills from leadership competency for the purpose of distinct definitions. These are skills that don't often get talked about unless you work in a fairly large organization that has at least some focus on career development. They're not always considered part of what great leaders do, but I consider them critical to long-term success. These survival skills include relationship building, coaching, mentoring and being mentored, building your network, promoting your achievements, and managing your career. I've found that mentoring in particular has been a great development tool for me because mentees often ask questions that either confirm my knowledge in a certain area or cause me to investigate something I don't know enough about. We will discuss each of these skills in more detail throughout the book, but suffice it to say here that a lot of it is about building and sustaining your career over the long haul. If you're not concerned about your career, don't expect anyone else to be.

Managing and leading people requires many skills.

You won't be able to master them all, nor should you, but you certainly should understand what you're good at and what you're not so good at. From there, either strengthen certain skills or hire or delegate accordingly for the things you don't do well but still need to do. Figure 1 outlines the categories of competencies that a manager needs to consider. Will you draw on skills from each of these daily? It's quite possible. Remember, your managerial duties go beyond single tasks. If you can demonstrate and develop skills in each area, you will find more success as a manager.

Micromanagement

I want to discuss micromanagement here because many managers do it. There are times when a manager starts a new assignment or project and gets into the details a bit more than is necessary, but when they become comfortable with the people they work with, know what everyone's role is, and see that everyone is contributing according to expectations, they will back off and take a more hands-off approach. This is different from blatant micromanagement, which actually impedes or undermines the activities of workers. Micromanagement happens when a manager closely watches and controls the work of subordinates. It often has a negative impact because micromanagers tend to be controlling, often to the level of bullying, which can limit productivity. It can also involve an excessive focus on smaller details, which leaves a manager unable to see or address larger (and often more important) details.

Being a micromanager often becomes an organizational death sentence for managers because they spend too much time worrying about every detail of everyone else's job and consequently forget about their own role. Arguably, the main job of managers is to use the resources they have been given to make sure assigned work gets completed. Micromanagement seems to be a problem of confidence; the manager might lack self-confidence and/or confidence in employees. In his May 7, 2012, guest post "How to Manage a Micromanager" on Deborah L. Jacobs' *Forbes* personal finance blog, Simon North describes a micromanager by writing, "This control freak is reluctant to delegate, may second-guess everything you do, and can shake your confidence in your own abilities." You don't want to adopt this as a management style, as it can be disastrous for your career. Be cautious about doing too much of other peoples' work. Remember, if you're doing their work, you're not doing your own. Trust that others are capable of performing their duties, and have faith that they might even accomplish more than you originally thought they could.

Good Manager, Good Leader

Getting things done through people requires good management skills, including the ability to plan, schedule, and organize work. A manager also needs to hire and train the right people to do the work at hand and to work in a safe manner. A manager needs to know when to take corrective action. In a sense, being a good manager means getting people to follow the established rules of the organization. Good leaders help people move beyond the established rules to perform above and beyond what is required. Some might call it the ability to motivate or engage, but whatever you call it, you will recognize it when you see it.

Managing people is a complex process because people are complex, and yet if we don't manage and lead them, they won't follow well. When I was working on this book, there was quite a bit of media attention in North America (and beyond) regarding sexual assault and misconduct in Hollywood. Producers, directors, and actors were at the centre of it, but as time went on and the momentum grew, people working in different industries and professions started coming forward.

One of the people accused was Patrick Brown, who at the time was the leader of the Progressive Conservative Party of Ontario. At the time of the writing of this book, nothing has been decided in the courts, but the court of public opinion resulted in his stepping down as leader, and this situation could have a negative impact on his political career for many years to come.

As the weeks passed, media coverage included Brown's defending himself publicly, denying and refuting the accusations against him, and even going to the extent of taking lie detector tests to prove his innocence. For the Ontario PC Party, the timing wasn't particularly good, as a provincial election was scheduled in four months. The PCs scrambled to find someone to lead the party and convince the people of Ontario that their party was the right choice to govern the province for the next four years. One might assume that chaos tore through the party's ranks, that tears and angst abounded, but as time went on, information started to emerge in the mainstream media indicating that perhaps not everyone in the party was sad to see Brown resign. It wasn't just related to the accusations of sexual misconduct levied against him; there were also concerns about his ability to lead. These concerns had apparently existed for some time. People in the party weren't happy about his leadership and were looking for any excuse to oust him from their most senior leadership position. I think some of the concerns were best captured by former Ontario PC MPP John Snobelen's commentary entitled "Brown Out," published in the *Toronto Sun* on March 2, 2018:

> Trust and loyalty are not leadership rights. Leaders must earn both. Brown simply failed to build the trust of his closest team, his caucus. [...]
> It is the job of leaders to show the way. To disrupt the status quo and cause a future. [...]
> It's good for leaders to be bold, to be ahead of the team. But it is hubris to believe that people must follow you and invest in your vision.

Great leaders never quit selling internally and externally.

These comments highlight the importance of leadership. Brown had lost the confidence of his caucus. If he hadn't, he might have received the support he would have needed to "weather the storm." He didn't get such support. He ended up resigning because most of his colleagues abandoned him. As Snobelen writes: "Make no mistake, Brown's demise was not simply the result of a single news report alleging character flaws. His leadership flaw was a failure to grasp the essential leadership imperative of continually building mutual respect and loyalty." Leaders simply cannot succeed without getting people to follow them, support them, and help them accomplish the work that needs to be completed.

The line between management and leadership is often blurred, and questions persist. Are they one and the same? Can a person be a good leader without being a manager? Can a person be a good manager but not a good leader? I think the answers to all of these questions can be yes when taken within certain contexts and depending on the definitions you use. If we use the context outlined above of the competencies regarding technical management and behavioural leadership and say that managers have only technical skills and leaders have only behavioural skills, then it's easy to separate the two. In reality, leaders usually have some of both. Does having more of one or the other make a manager a better manager or a leader a better leader? Possibly, but it all depends on how the person uses them. Do they use them for good to advance the organization and the careers of others or do they use them only to advance their own agendas?

Over the past forty-two years that I have been in business, I have met managers who have become fairly successful even though they used questionable methods and, in some cases, unethical means. As a manager, you might wrestle with this yourself as you progress in your career. We as a society have in many ways abandoned our values and integrity and allowed people to govern from senior positions simply because they were good at developing business, were good salespeople, or were good at getting votes or making movies or growing the company.

You need to decide how you will lead.

Will you lead from a platform of good character? This includes honesty, respect, and integrity. Or will you lead with only your own personal self-interest in mind? This usually means having little concern about the careers of others or the success of the organization you work for.

Will you give more than you take? Building up other people and the organization will require great effort on your part. Or will you forgo great leadership and manage with the bare minimum in mind? Not many managers I know want to be remembered as a mediocre manager, and they certainly don't want it on their tombstone.

It's up to you to determine what kind of manager and what kind of leader you will be.

Chapter 2

From Deckhand to Captain: Transitioning from Individual Contributor to Manager

Finally the day arrives. Someone has decided that you have the skills to be the skipper of your own ship. You have progressed beyond deckhand, a noble profession in and of itself, to a position where you oversee the activities of others. Maybe you planned for this to happen all the way along and have been preparing for this day.

There's an old story that goes like this. Two old salts are aboard a ship one day, and one says to the other, "So tell me. How did you end up a member of this ship's crew?" The other one says, "Well, when I was younger, I knew I wanted to go to sea and someday become the captain of my own boat, so I read every book I could about sailing. An opportunity came up for me to become a cabin boy, and from there I became a deckhand and then second mate and then first mate of this great ship. What about you?" The first man, who was the captain of the ship, says, "Well, one night I was drunk in a bar down by the docks. When I left, someone threw a bag over my head, and I woke up the next morning in the hold of a tramp steamer. I worked my way up from there."

The moral of the story? Sometimes you find a job, and sometimes it finds you.

The Tap on the Shoulder

I've heard many leaders share the story of how they got their first job in management. Although some leaders had definite career aspirations towards management, more often than not, moving into management is unplanned or unexpected. Many were tapped on the shoulder and asked about their desire to move into management. Others were simply told they were moving into management on the following Monday. In this chapter, we will explore some of the factors that influence new managers as they begin the voyage from individual contributor to self-aware, goal-oriented manager. The following is a true story about a young manager I met while consulting in the nineties.

Susan joined the local hospital after completing her nursing program at a prestigious university. After working for a couple of years, doing the three-shift rotations, she realized that she wanted to do more than just provide direct patient care. She thought she might want to go into administration. She signed up for a master's program in health care administration at a local university, which she completed three years later at the age of twenty-six. She accomplished this by taking a steady night shift so she could attend day classes.

She knew she wanted more, so she was surprised by how nervous she felt when she was presented with an offer of more. She twisted and squirmed in the chair when Miranda, the chief of nursing, offered her a supervisor's position. One of Susan's colleagues was leaving for a one-year maternity leave, and she had to leave unexpectedly early because of health complications. Susan appreciated the offer and realized it wasn't something she could easily refuse, but the suddenness of it frightened her.

Miranda expressed every confidence in Susan's ability to do the job and reminded her that she was one of the department's top performers. (Susan always completed her work on time to the highest standards.) Miranda even noted that she thought Susan had what it took to be a great leader. She also pointed out that the position was temporary, that Susan would always be welcomed back to her current position if things didn't work out, and that it would be a great learning opportunity regardless. Susan certainly didn't want to disappoint her boss. She agreed that it was a great opportunity and that she would welcome the challenge.

Miranda was pleased and promised to let their team know about the change on Monday morning. She told Susan to think about anything she would like to say to the team following the announcement.

As Susan drove home from work, she wondered how other people in the department would react to Miranda's decision to appoint her as supervisor. Susan knew that other people in the department were interested in pursuing management positions and hadn't been given the opportunity. She wondered if everyone really liked her, as Miranda had suggested, because she remembered experiencing occasional disagreements with two of the staff.

Susan also wondered what kind of supervisor she would be. She knew from her management studies at university that there were different styles such as autocratic, consultative, participative, and transformational, and she felt she needed to know what style she would demonstrate from day one.

As Susan opened the door of her car in her driveway, she realized that no one had ever asked her that question and that she had never really given it any serious thought. She headed for the front door, realizing that it was going to be a long weekend.

Maybe you can relate to Susan's story. Maybe you've been promoted from an individual contributor role. Maybe you're regarded as a high performer with potential. Maybe you've been included in special projects because of your performance or have served in a temporary supervisory role. Maybe you're simply considered the best at what you do from a technical aspect.

When you accept a management position, you essentially accept that your job will change from completing tasks yourself to completing tasks through other people. This can be a very difficult transition for new managers. Why? Many new managers feel that no one can do a job quite as well as they can (and they often get in the way of productivity as a result). Others feel more competent in their former role of "doer" and less competent in their new role as coach, mentor, and advisor. In simple terms, many people don't know how to be a manager or leader and don't understand how their role has changed.

It's Not Me; It's the Position

Some employees will be a joy and an honour to work with. Others will challenge you or will part company with you to find their true calling. Regardless of the situation, you will encounter many experiences in your managerial role that relate more to your position than to you as a person. As a leader, you may need to make some unpopular decisions regarding layoffs, hiring and firing, rescheduling, and assignment changes, all of which can create waves for you to navigate. Don't take it personally! There's a saying I heard once when I was starting out in business: "At any given time, two out of three people who work for you will hate you." Why? Because you're the boss.

Understanding Your Influence

Developing yourself and others is essential to leadership success. Your voyage toward success isn't a solitary one. Your personal, professional, and organizational goals may vary, but to succeed as a manager, you must use the human resources at your disposal to accomplish specific tasks and goals.

In his book *The 21 Irrefutable Laws of Leadership*, John Maxwell states the impact of leadership quite clearly: "If you don't have influence, you will never be able to lead others." This is an important concept to remember because, as we have come to realize, positional authority in North America based strictly on the power one can exert over employees in many of today's white-collar jobs doesn't carry as much weight as it did before 1990. Quite frankly, people aren't as willing to put up with the crap they used to from egocentric, autocratic types prone to harassment. Today, employees are more educated, mobile, and worldly, and other organizations will pursue them if they're good at what they do. While there are jobs available elsewhere for high-end positions, employees won't want to work for someone they don't respect or regard as a good leader.

It's important to note that this refers more to white-collar positions. Unfortunately, with the continued shrinking manufacturing base in Canada and the US, many workers feel powerless when trying to maintain a well-paid manufacturing position that's otherwise hard to come by. This means they are more likely to put up with the poor behaviour that some organizations and their representatives exhibit. In some cases, unions have been able to counteract this by protecting workers and their rights in larger organizations.

Various strategies can help you influence someone in a positive way. Think about the people who have influenced you, such as teachers, coaches, community leaders, business leaders, family members, celebrities, and political figures. Are they experts in their field? Do you respect their position in their community? Do you admire or desire their accomplishments? Have they helped you develop yourself in a meaningful way?

Think about the influence these people have over your decisions. Now realize that those people rarely have direct power over you. If that's the case, how do these people influence you and how do you influence others?

I believe that influence is important because it's rooted in our free will. When someone influences us, we aren't made to do something contrary to our beliefs or desires. We're influenced to do something of our own volition. It's our choice to follow the examples of these people. A person who has been influenced and is in an empowered position becomes increasingly inspired and becomes more committed and willing to tackle new challenges. As a manager, influencing your employees in a positive manner often translates into greater productivity, higher quality work, better customer service, and a more satisfied workforce.

Influence goes beyond your employees. You can also influence your peers and your bosses. These are people you don't have any positional authority over, so you have to use influencing techniques that don't rely on the position you hold. In their book *Influence without Authority*, Allan R. Cohen and David L. Bradford have even suggested that "nobody has the formal authority to achieve what is necessary, not even with those who report to them. It is an illusion that once upon a time managers could make their direct reports do whatever was needed. Nobody has ever had that authority—they never have and never will." As such, you need to rely on your skills of influence. Certainly, a big part of this means understanding what your employees need and want and then influencing them accordingly to help facilitate the change you need.

For illustrative purposes, I would like to tell a personal story of how I had to influence my manager at an early point in my career. I started reporting to a new senior manager who had just joined the organization after completing several other successful postings at very senior levels across Canada. I was just one of several managers who would be reporting to her, and there was a lot of anxiety amongst the group before she arrived. Everyone wondered what she would be like, whether she wanted to make all kinds of changes, whether she would bring in her own people, and generally what kind of leader she would be. Everyone started to plan their own approaches, which isn't uncommon under these circumstances as a strategy for self-preservation. My own thoughts were less about survival, as I was young and had other job opportunities. I liked this organization and had been able to advance some of my own ideas, so I was thinking more about how I could influence this new manager to continue to support my ideas and hence my advancement in the organization.

My approach was fairly simple. I wanted to find out as much as possible about her decision-making process and how I could influence her to support my initiatives. After some early discussions with other colleagues who had already met with her and a couple of initial meetings I had with her, I found out that she was a bottom-line, to-the-point manager. She was honest and straightforward and needed to know a project's required research and supporting documents but didn't necessarily want to get dragged into the details. She wanted to be very detailed in making sure the backup work had been done. This was very painful for me to learn, as I hated detail work and usually assigned tasks requiring extreme attention to detail to a member of my operating group who loved the world of spreadsheets, future projections, research, etc. But I needed her to have confidence in my recommendations. I realized that I was going to have to spend a bit more time in the minutiae than I typically did so I could provide the level of comfort my new manager needed.

So I did. When I went into her office for meetings or to present a case, I would provider her with reams of data, often carrying in three or four thick file folders with all the supporting documents. I would sometimes bring in the one of my staff who had done some of the work on collecting the information to legitimize the details even more. I made sure I could speak about all the information so I could give her the confidence she needed to make the decision. I didn't always get what I wanted, but I was always prepared.

In the early stages of our relationship, I had to go through a lot of details, showing her graphs and spreadsheets and comparative research. After about three months, however, she began asking less and less about the supporting documents. Then one day she simply asked me, "What's the bottom line?" I had been able to build enough trust that my team and I would do all the necessary supporting documents that she didn't need to ask for the details anymore, which she had already admitted she didn't like any more than I did. She could now focus on the bottom line in my case, which is what I wanted. I had been able to influence her by giving her the details she needed.

I should note that I still took a big file folder full of papers to every meeting in the future. That way whenever she said, "I know you've done all the preparation of the supporting documents," I would just pat the folder and assure her that it was all there.

Influence is an incredibly important aspect of what managers do. There is some good material on this subject that I advise new managers to read. Along with the above-mentioned *Influence without Authority*, another important book is Robert Cialdini's seminal book *Influence: The Psychology of Persuasion*. It's worth taking a look at these two books, as they provide some essential techniques and strategies on influence.

Influencing through Change

Influencing people to accept your ideas and recommendations is an important aspect of any manager's job and will certainly enhance the chances of your success, but even more important is your ability to influence as it relates to change. As we know, constant change is now the norm. This is in large part due to today's rapid pace of new information and new ideas. Being able to adapt to change has become a necessity, and managers play a key role in helping employees acknowledge, understand, and execute new initiatives.

The book *Influencer: The New Science of Leading Change* by Joseph Grenny et al. engages the reader in all aspects of influence and change. The authors discuss the change agent as the "influencer" and detail several stories about these people and how they influence change. They outline three key elements of influence, which they describe in simple terms as follows:

1. *Focus and measure*. Influencers know exactly what they want and are "zealous" about measuring it.

2. *Find vital behaviours*. Influencers focus on two or three behaviours that will get them the greatest change results.

3. *Engage all six sources of influence*. Influencers need to get people to adopt the new behaviours. The authors point out that this is no easy task. The idea is that rather then engage only one or two areas of influence, they recommend engaging all six areas that they have identified: personal motivation, personal ability, social motivation, social ability, structural motivation, and structural ability.

To give you a sense of the effect that behaviours can have, I would like to share a story from Caren Burt, my wife and colleague. Caren is a management consultant and leadership coach with years of experience advising and coaching managers at all levels within organizations.

I was working with a new manager who was only in her early twenties and was already put in a position of significant responsibility. After she spent a year in the role, her employee engagement scores were miles ahead of the rest of the organization. The pay, the jobs, and the workplaces were all similar and yet there was such a disparity between her area and other similar areas managed by other people. What was this person, who was younger and less experienced, doing? It simply came down to a lot of common sense and respect for people.

Using humility and generosity is how I would describe her approach. She listened to her employees and removed barriers for them to help make them more effective and therefore more satisfied in their work. Her people were passionate and hardworking, and she gave them the opportunity to make decisions. When they expressed a desire to make shift changes, she would let them create the schedule and try it out. They were committed to it, and if it didn't work out, I'm sure they would find a solution.

People want to have as much autonomy in their work as possible, but this can sometimes be a challenge, especially in a highly regulated industry, so she searched for ways to give them autonomy where it wouldn't interfere with compliance or customer service. She gets out of her office and knows what's going on. She asks questions and provides coaching and feedback. Self-reflection can be hard on people, but I believe her greatest achievement in her career thus far is her ability to self-reflect with humility and listen to her people.

Caren shared story after story with me about successful managers she had worked with over the years who managed and led people through their good character. This is what I described above as leadership behaviour rather than management skills. In this case, it was this young manager's ability to self-reflect with humility and listen to her people that led to her success. She also was prepared to coach her employees and give them some autonomy.

Leading people well requires more than just showing up for work and telling people what to do. It's about finding ways to engage your employees so that their work becomes more than just a means to earn an income. Engaged employees look at their jobs as something to take pride in, especially when they feel their work has an impact on the organization, whether it's installing parts on automobiles, emailing clients, dealing with disgruntled customers, or sweeping the floors at NASA's space centre.

Chapter 3

Plotting Your Course: Building a Management Platform

If you don't know your destination, it will be difficult to plot your course. I often ask clients this question as part of my professional coaching practice: What do you want to build over the next two to five years? This is a critical question for any manager even if the answer is as simple as "I want to build my experience as a manager so I'm ready for the next level." I'm always surprised when new managers tell me they haven't thought about this and that the only thing they've thought about was "not screwing up." That's not necessarily a bad answer, but when I ask them how they plan on doing that, their faces often draw a worried look. In this chapter, we will discuss ways to plot your course and avoid critical mistakes in the early stages of your new role as a manager.

What Do You Want to Build?

One of the more difficult challenges for new managers is the transition from individual contributor to manager. It often requires you to let go of knowing and doing the job directly and instead depends on your ability to see the bigger picture. What do success and happiness look like to you? Are you able to look beyond your former role as an individual contributor? Can you see the potential of the human resources you now manage? There's a story about President John F. Kennedy touring the NASA space centre, where he happened upon a custodian sweeping the floor. Kennedy naively asked the man what he was doing. The custodian's response caught him off guard: "Mr. President, I'm helping put a man on the moon."

Let's define some motivations and identify some personal and professional goals. When coaching new or aspiring managers, I always ask them why they want to be a manager and what they want to achieve. I ask them to consider their bigger picture. Some of the answers I have received include the following:

- I want to make a difference.
- I want to make this a better place to work.
- I'm ready for the next stage in my career.
- I want to be in charge.
- I want to make more money.
- I don't like the way things are done around here; I have some better ideas.

If you want to become a successful leader, you need to think about why you're drawn to that role. Most of the reasons for wanting to become a leader aren't bad, but some more than others may lead you to greater success. For example, if your only reason for moving into management is to make more money, you may struggle more than those whose goal is to make the organization a better place to work. In other words, there's a degree of self-analysis required when considering a move into management.

If you work best alone, like to do all the work yourself, and feel that others can't do the work as well as you can, then you demonstrate the characteristics of an individual contributor rather than the characteristics of a good manager. If this is how you operate and your main motivator is monetary reward, then a move into management could have disastrous consequences for your career, for the careers of the people around you, and for your organization.

It's important to consider how you work and how you view the work of others. This type of self-analysis will help you understand what you're good at and what you're not so good at (i.e., your strengths and weaknesses). It will also help you articulate to your subordinates, peers, and superiors what you're about and what you're trying to build in the future as a new or aspiring manager. This way everyone will understand what they need to do to support you and how you can all work together efficiently to help you meet your goals. Think about some of these questions:

- Do you feel greater satisfaction completing a task yourself or seeing others do the work?
- Do you feel you can do a better job than anyone else?

- Do you enjoy delegating work so you can move on to more important tasks?
- Do you enjoy collaborating and involving people in the work you do?
- Are you comfortable allowing people to receive credit for the work they do?

One of the strategies I started employing about ten years ago is what I call the first two weeks and the first three months. A focus on the first two weeks was born out of a question that recruiters seem to use quite regularly. It usually goes something like this: "So what will you do for the first week or two in your new job?" However, the first three months occurred to me from companies that adopted ninety-day cycles to focus on increased sales, increased customers, or revenue generation. I decided these would be great planning time frames for new managers, whether first-time managers or experienced managers moving to a new department, division, or company. What I realized right away was that many of the concerns are related to communication.

When a new manager joins a department, there is usually a lot of confusion and excitement for both the manager and the employees, and there will be a lot of questions on people's minds. Whether these questions are answered and whether people believe the answers are honest and open will determine the working relationship between the staff and their new boss. The questions on the employees' minds may include:

- What is this person like?
- Do I trust this person?
- What is their management style?
- What will they do if I make a mistake?
- Will they ask for my opinion?
- Will they want to change things (job descriptions, the department's workflow, etc.)?
- How will any changes affect me (change in job duties, different hours, etc.)?

You as the manager may have similar questions:

- What are these people like?
- Do I trust them and do they trust me?
- How were they managed in the past compared to my management style?
- What will I do if someone makes a mistake?
- How will they react if I ask for their opinions?
- Do I want to change things?
- How will they react if I change things?
- How will managing this group affect me?

After observing new managers over the past few decades, I've come to realize that these time frames are an important place for them to start because they can focus on them to make adequate plans and take actions that will have a significant impact.

The First Two Weeks

If you're set to begin your new job as a manager on

Monday, you're probably running the questions above through your mind over and over again, thinking about how that first day will go, but you should be thinking about the first two weeks. I refer to this first period as "getting to know me and getting to know you" time. Let's look at the key elements a new manager needs to address in the first two weeks in order to increase the chances for success in the new role.

Hold a High-Level Meeting (or Two) with All Staff

This is where you can introduce yourself, including where you come from, why you're excited to be there, and what you're going to be doing in the first two weeks. You can use this time to outline the one-on-one meetings you will be conducting with all staff in the future.

This is also where you can begin to talk about who you are as a leader. This is the initial conversation you'll have with people as a way to let them in. They will get to know you and understand your management style and what kind of leader you will be. For example, you may want to communicate to them that you prefer to lead from a perspective of support, from a place of openness and honesty, with an ongoing open-door policy, etc.

Your goal here is to initiate the building of trust. You want to let the staff know that they can trust you with important information that they choose to share with you. For example, maybe they will come up with an idea of how to make things better. Remember that employees who have been in the organization for a long time often have the best ideas on how to improve it.

Meet with Your Executive Assistant (If You Have One)
Meet with your executive assistant so you will understand what they will be doing to support you. Also find out what information they require from you.

If you're fortunate enough to have administrative support staff, they can play an important role in your success. They often know many of the people in the organization—not only your staff but also peers and superiors. They can often help you avoid the landmines that new managers typically step on. They can also help you understand what the company culture is really like. Perhaps most importantly, they will provide a lot of the administrative support functions that will allow you to do what you need to do, which is focus on your staff.

Hold One-on-One Meetings with Each Staff Member
Once you've held larger group meetings and you've met with your administrative support, you can start to hold your one-on-one meetings with your direct reports. If you're lucky, you will be able to complete these within the first two weeks. However, if you have to hold more than ten of these meetings, you may need to spread them out over a longer period.

These meetings will provide you with the opportunity to introduce yourself again on a more personal level. They will also allow you to go into more detail about your management style, your coaching style, your plans for the first three months, and your long-term vision if you've prepared that by this point. You may also wish to ask the employee what you need to do to make things better. They may not have an answer at that time, but you can ask them to think about it for your next meeting with them.

This is also an opportunity to get to know the employee by gathering some basic background information. You can learn about their role, what they're most proud of, and what their concerns are (if any). You can communicate your expectations to them and what they can expect from you. You may not have an answer for every question an employee asks you, but this at least begins a dialogue for future conversations.

At the conclusion of each meeting, let the employee know when their next meeting will be, whether it's next week, next a month, or next quarter. Regardless, it's important to set up a follow-up meeting for your next discussion.

Reading manuals, past reports, production spreadsheets, budget statements etc., is very important for a new manager to do. You will need to do it at some point, and early on you might find yourself going through these materials on evenings and weekends. This is fine because one of the best ways to get to know the organization is though meeting people during regular work hours.

Meet with your boss early on to make sure you are both clear on certain deliverables and time frames. Perhaps you will have already met with your new boss by the time you start your new role, or maybe you scheduled this meeting on the first day. However, if it hasn't taken place yet, it's important to get around to it sooner rather than later so you will have a clear understanding of your boss' expectations.

Your boss probably already has a good sense of your management style, as this was likely a topic during the interviews and/or discussions regarding your promotion or recruitment, and you may already have asked about their own management style. You can use this meeting to ask follow-up questions about this or to clear up any confusion. You will also want to determine how often you will meet with them. Finally, this is a great opportunity to ask if there is anyone else in the organization you should meet with. This could be anyone who may ultimately assist you with your job.

The First Three Months

If the first two weeks are about your getting to know your direct reports and their getting to know you, the first three months is about getting to know the business. You may already have a good idea about the technical side of the business, and maybe that's why you were hired as a manager, but now you need to understand your specific area of operations so you can maintain operations where necessary, make changes where appropriate, and inspire and engage staff to get things done. Let's look at the key elements a new manager needs to address in the first three months.

Assess Your Team's Current Strengths and Opportunities
At this point, you will have had most (if not all) of your one-on-one meetings with individual staff members and will have a sense of their strengths. You may have received some feedback from them on areas for improvement. You will have also observed the operations for a while and reviewed productivity and quality reports to consider some ideas for improvement. During this time, you will have also had a chance to meet with your boss to discuss expectations and areas for improvement. This isn't necessarily when you'll make all the changes, but you will at least start to formulate a plan you will execute over the next six to twelve months with the agreement of your manager.

Develop a Communication Strategy for Your Team
This is often overlooked. We often assume a communication strategy isn't necessary, as we can just tell people the things they need to know when they need to hear them. I suggest developing a proper communication strategy to ensure you get either critical or general information to the right people on a timely and secure basis. It can be something as simple as monthly team meetings, quarterly meetings, or an internal newsletter.

A friend of mine who manages a high-performing sales group recently employed a new communication strategy. She had been conducting one-on-one meetings with her staff of seven for some time, but she felt that those meetings were becoming more operational and reactive. Although they were generally good and she wanted to continue them, what she needed was short, high-energy, regular meetings that anyone on her team could participate in regardless of where they were. This is made possible by the technology available today. Now people can participate in meetings in person, over the phone, over streaming video, etc.

Some organizations call this kind of meeting "team huddles," but she prefers the name "hot buttons and heartburn." The idea is that everybody on the team gets a chance to join in the conversation, which takes place first thing on Monday mornings. They talk about any critical issues that have come up and that they will be dealing with over the coming week. This is what she has to say about the meetings:

> It gives everyone on the team an idea of what other critical things people are working on, especially when they aren't available for a meeting, appointment, or call they previously planned. It's part of the idea of transparent leadership. The whole idea is that our colleagues and employees actually have an idea what we're working on, and it maybe helps avoid that long-standing comment employees make about their boss: "I don't know what they do all day."

It also really helps me keep up to speed on what people are doing. Things change so fast and priorities change. It's easy for me to lose track of what people are actively engaged in beyond their regular activities. We also get a chance to share some quick good news stories, which really help build confidence and remind people of the great work we do. It's like thirty minutes and then we're back at it.

Schedule Individual and Team Meetings for the Next Six Months

Setting up meetings well in advance is important. People need to know that there is a set time for you to meet to discuss issues. Outline an agenda for each meeting so people can prepare for them. These meetings may include discussions about goals and objectives, progress updates, personal training and development opportunities, and performance reports. They may also include brainstorming sessions and good news stories from both you and your employees.

These sessions don't need to be longer than half an hour, but it's important to set an agenda and stick to it. Don't bother holding a meeting if all you're going to do is ask, "So tell me what's going on?" Effective meetings need more substance. They need to provide value because they remove people from their daily work routine. Don't let regular meetings become little more than a waste of people's time.

There will always be someone who claims that

meetings are a waste of time. In many cases it's true. Poor planning leads to meetings that go nowhere because there's no set purpose or planned outcome. Yet employees are probably the most important and expensive resource you have. If you're not spending time with them, where are you spending your time?

Meet with Your Boss Regularly

It shouldn't come as a surprise that regularly meeting with your boss is critical to your success. At the very least, meet with your boss to outline findings and provide action plans for next six months. It's also a chance for you to highlight your team's accomplishments and to continually recalibrate what your boss' expectations are. This will help you keep on target.

Your boss may not be very good at scheduling this time with you, so don't be afraid to help them out by suggesting frequency, topics, and outcomes. One thing I have told my direct reports over the past thirty years is, "Don't let me get caught with my pants down." In other words, if you're changing something—introducing a new process or modifying an existing one, for example—make sure you let me know. That way, if my boss, a peer, or an employee asks me about it, I can respond knowingly rather than simply give them a confused look and shrug my shoulders. Use these meetings to give your boss a heads-up on changes you're considering so they don't get blindsided later on.

Finally, be sure to meet one-on-one with the peers, senior executives, and specialists such as IT, finance, legal, and HR personnel you may regularly interact with in your role. You generally want to meet with any "internal customers," the people you support and the people who support you.

It's important to establish relationships with such people early on. In the last permanent position I applied for and was successful at landing, I identified fifty-seven people in addition to my direct reports that I wanted to meet within the first three months. These were mainly internal customers and specialists who provided critical internal support to my operational group. The meetings were sometimes just a quick hello to introduce myself, but in other meetings, I had specific questions about the services we were providing and offered my assistance in improving them. This established a relationship so people would have a direct line to me if problems arose as opposed to people going over my head to my boss.

It also worked better for me to meet people one-on-one before engaging them in larger multi-departmental meetings dealing with critical issues. For example, when meeting with a peer for the first time (let's call him Pete), he told me he was having some difficulty with one of my direct reports. There was an issue with getting information for a critical project Pete's group was working on, so he was going to bring it up at his next project management meeting. By meeting with

Pete beforehand and getting a heads-up on the problem, I was able to find out what was holding up the information coming out of my department. It was a simple conflict of priorities, and I corrected the situation. When Pete went to his project management meeting, he reported that my department had worked very quickly and thoroughly to resolve the issue instead of reporting that my department was a roadblock. That was a great outcome versus a potentially embarrassing one that could have arisen during a large meeting with different departments in attendance, not to mention my boss and several other senior managers.

A Great Start

Without a doubt, the first two weeks and first three months are critical periods for the new manager. You essentially use this time to gain a foothold, especially if you're new to the organization. These periods will produce what will be your first impression in your new role as a manager. Although I have laid out the key elements above, you will likely end up working on all kinds of things in addition to them. You will probably be expected to hit the ground running with the operation of your group. You will have to attend meetings, read and write reports, deal with employee issues, start new projects, recruit new team members, etc. Let me assure you that if you don't get the relationship meetings underway during these initial periods, you never will because things will just get busier. You may have an idea of how your new role will play out, but in reality, things never settle down.

I remember reading an article back in the eighties that suggested certain people would be able to shift to a four-day workweek by the late nineties. The idea was that the advent of computers would change the world by reducing and speeding up much of the administrative work we were currently doing manually. However, with more information comes more work, and people are still working five-day workweeks three decades later. Actually, many of us work more after hours than ever before. My point is that things will continue to grow in complexity. There will always be a need to do things more effectively and efficiently, which usually means doing more work with fewer people. You need to take the opportunity to meet with people and build many relationships early on because you will come to depend on many people in the future.

During these initial periods of gathering information, you're also confirming or getting a better idea of what it is you want to accomplish, whether it's better customer service, improved product quality, faster delivery times, or increased access to information. Remember, the work you need to get done relies on the people you have as resources, whether they report directly to you or have an indirect relationship with you.

In this chapter, we've covered some key components for the new manager to consider. First, why do you want to be a manager? Are you driven by money and power? Or is there some higher cause? This requires a bit of a self-analysis, and it will take you to different places depending on what motivates you. Maybe several things motivate you. Whatever it is, knowing yourself as a manager is a continuing journey. Why is this important? If you continue to seek out new opportunities, it's good to find ones that best match who you are. If, for example, you're looking for advancement in an organization in a certain field and you choose an organization that has only two people in your chosen area, you might find it difficult to advance. This can be frustrating. If, on the other hand, you're mostly interested in serving a higher cause such as being environmentally respectful and you choose an organization with a disastrous environmental record, this may also create tremendous conflict in you.

Once you understand yourself and where you want to be, it comes down to taking advantage of the first phase of your new role as manager. Once you've established yourself within the organization, you can look forward to bigger things.

Leaving Port: Casting Off the Lines and Heading Out to Sea

It's finally time to leave the safety and security of the harbour. You've been tied up securely to the pier. You've gotten to know the condition of the ship and the state of your crew. You've received lots of support and advice, but your ship and crew haven't had to worry about the tides and the weather yet. You haven't had an opportunity to try out your navigational skills and test what you've learned in preparation.

As you cast off the lines and the maneuvering thrusters start to push you away from the pier, you realize you're heading out to sea. You ask yourself whether you've adequately prepared everything for the voyage. What are some of the final checks you'll need to make before hitting the open sea? You're heading to an area where immediate help will be less available. Now you'll have to rely on your own skills and those of your crew.

Chapter 4

The Masts and Ropes of Your Sails: Communication

The personnel on cruise ships make all kinds of efforts to communicate with passengers, whether it's the next day's agenda dropped in a file holder outside your cabin each evening, the endless announcements about upcoming events, or what to do in the event of an emergency. These ships have access to the Internet, and of course passengers can make phone calls either with their cellphone or with the phone in their stateroom. I remember watching old movies where ships used flags and signal lamps to send messages from ship to ship or sometimes to people on shore.

We have come a long way in our ability to communicate. This is why it amuses me when managers struggle with communicating information to their subordinates. Every book on management seems to include the topic of communication somewhere. There are different names for it, including "understanding your employees," "asking powerful questions," "the art of conversation," and "developing your listening skills," but at the heart of all these fancy terms is the essence of communication.

Managers are always trying to find more effective ways to communicate with their employees. Add onto this the research revealing that certain communication styles work better than others depending on the person and the situation. For example, some people prefer to communicate in a more collegial way. This is where you address a subordinate more like a peer than a subordinate. Others prefer collaborative relationships where you as the boss seek out ideas or feedback on your ideas. Some people respond best to a directive style, where you simply tell them what to do. The secret to success with any of these styles is knowing your employees and which style they respond best to. From there, be consistent and be timely in applying these styles.

Based on my experience and certainly on what I have heard through my consulting practice, most managers at some point struggle with communicating to their employees, whether it's regarding goals and expectations, performance, disciplinary measures, motivation, decision-making, or the many other conversations that take place in the workplace. In this chapter, we will discuss three key elements of communication:

1. clarity
2. listening
3. the honest conversation

All the great leaders I have had the opportunity to

work with or meet have had one thing in common: They get their message through to the people who need to receive it, whether it's to a large group or an individual, whether it's verbal or written. Great leaders know best how to communicate important information regardless of the receiver or the method.

Maintain Clarity in Communication

It's essential to have clarity in communication. This means ensuring that you and your co-workers understand each other's messages at a basic level. It also means setting and communicating clear and attainable expectations based on your personal, professional, and organizational goals. Establishing clear and attainable expectations is something we often overlook. We assume that people understand what their job is and how it contributes to larger organizational goals simply because they've done the job for a long time.

Your employees will often understand what their primary role is in the organization, but they're less likely to understand how their role fits into the larger picture. For example, they may be confused about how their activities affect the departments with which they exchange information or anything essential to the operation of the business. This lack of understanding may be rooted in unclear communication, and it can lead to the breakdown of external and internal customer service chains.

Many people just don't realize how their actions affect others. In some cases, employees aren't held accountable for poor performance or outcomes. When that happens, companies can suffer tremendous losses. When the large automotive companies in North America allowed quality and pricing to get away from them in the seventies and eighties, customers took matters into their own hands. The influx of lower cost, higher quality fuel-efficient cars from foreign companies changed the automotive industry forever. If organizations and their employees don't pay attention to their products and services, their customers will.

It has become apparent to me over the years that organizations tend to get into trouble when management and employees stop talking to each other and finding solutions together. As already mentioned, solutions to internal issues often lie with the people closest to the work, which is usually the people actually performing the work. Moreover, meaningful conversations with employees don't normally happen by chance. They have to be planned, scheduled, and conducted. Genuine discussions need to take place and they need to include action plans, desired outcomes, and constructive feedback.

When I start a new job, I always meet with each employee in the department in one-on-one meetings. It's an opportunity for me to talk about what I want to accomplish, but more importantly it's a chance for me to start getting to know them, to find out what they do, and to check whether they understand how they contribute to the organization. From that point, for future meetings I can plan what additional clarity I need to provide to them. For example, I can provide additional information during regular checkpoints and performance meetings. I realize that the primary excuse for avoiding such meetings is "no time." If you can't spend fifteen to thirty minutes a month to check in with the people who are actually providing the products or services to your customers, you may need to re-evaluate your personal and professional goals. Consider these questions when thinking about how to communicate and clarify expectations with your employees:

1. Do you have regular one-on-one meetings with each of your employees?

    I have always found these extremely useful but only if there's an agenda. This can be something as simple as an update on key projects, goals, development opportunities, and good news stories. Managers can use fairly simple questions such as "What went well?" "What didn't go so well?" "What would you change?" and "What did you learn?" On the other hand, you might update the employee on sales forecasts, inform them of any changes that might affect them, or brief them on relevant information regarding other operating units that report to you.

2. Have you checked in with employees about what their job is and how it contributes to the bigger picture?

Role clarity and reinforcement are critical parts of a manager's job. Roles are often expanded without anyone recognizing the increased responsibility. More responsibility doesn't necessarily mean more compensation, but it should include a discussion to determine how any changes will affect the employee's current list of priorities. I've seen instances where job descriptions were years out of date or where employees were doing work that their boss stopped managing years ago. In one case, employees were manually preparing extensive reports for their manager that the manager no longer used; the manager was accessing information through a new management information system but had neglected to tell employees.

People tend to work better when they understand how their work contributes to the organization. Like the custodian at NASA who told President Kennedy he was helping put a man on the moon, do the people who report to you understand where they fit in the grand scheme of things?

3. What are your personal, professional, and organizational goals and how do they relate to your employees?

This is something that managers often don't consider. Either they're too busy or they don't think it's important enough. Sometimes managers get around to doing this only after a crisis such as being fired, receiving a scathing report about their department after an employee survey, or getting a visit from their boss regarding a downturn in business and changes that need to be made.

As managers, we should be constantly thinking about and assessing the contributions we make to the organization on an individual and departmental level and how we can continually develop our managerial and leadership skills. A simple test is that if you regularly achieve success and are always finding other career opportunities both within and outside the organization, then you are clearly adding value.

The Importance of Listening

I recently conducted a survey with a group of human resources professionals. I posed questions in several different areas. One question addressed the issue of the top critical behaviours that a manager needs to exhibit to build credibility and trust. The number one response was *listening*. This might seem surprising to some, but it wasn't to me. We get caught up in the idea that employees are looking for some complex array of skills, but it starts with something very simple: listening in a way that signals to the employee that they are being heard.

While I was writing this book, I did a quick search on Amazon to get a sense of how many titles they had listed on "effective listening skills." They had 104 current titles. This, of course, didn't include books they didn't have listed. As you can see, there are lots of resources out there for anyone looking for techniques to enhance their listening skills. From this alone, we get a sense that this in an important topic.

From my perspective and from questions I have asked managers and leaders, listening is certainly an important component of communication. More importantly, it's a critical factor in your ability to influence people as a leader. If you do nothing else from an interpersonal perspective, listen well, listen with intent, and listen to gain understanding. Over the years, I have observed what I believe are the three different levels of listening:

1. *Listening on the surface.* You listen to the words and accept them, but you don't dig any deeper or search for clarification.

2. *Listening in the middle.* You hear and accept the words but also ask for clarification or use active listening skills.

3. *Investigative listening.* You listen well but also recognize that there is more of a story behind the words or between the lines. You seek to understand things on a deeper level. You read body language and interpret inflections.

Each of these levels of listening is important, and different levels can be used at different times. Although the third level is the most in depth, you shouldn't always aim to use that level of listening—time and energy simply won't permit it. However, I find that people aren't always listening even when they indicate they are. The following is an example of what I mean.

A few years ago, I was out golfing with Jerry, the husband of a dear friend of mine, Jolin. As we strolled around the course, we had many discussions. I was fascinated by how Jerry responded to many of the statements I made. He often responded with, "I hear you." When we returned home after golfing, I had a chance to chat privately with Jolin. She asked how the day went and what I thought of her husband, as I had only just met Jerry. I said, "I think we had a great day, and I appreciated the insightful conversations we had." To that, Jolin said, "That's great because Jerry can get bored and distracted very easily and won't listen to anything, and when he does that, he responds to everything with, 'I hear you.'"

Listen well. Listen with intent. Listen to gain understanding.

I've pointed out that there are many books on improving communication and listening skills. Many of them probably cover the subject in a lot more detail than I can, but if you have neither the time nor the inclination to get into heavier reading, I would suggest at least asking yourself the following questions. These questions will help guide you in the right direction for having more meaningful conversations with your employees.

1. When you speak with an employee, do you listen to and acknowledge what they say?

2. Do you set aside time to have a conversation with them without smartphones or other devices interfering? I refer to this as being present.

3. Do you ask them questions for clarification and to better understand them?

4. Do you take notes and make eye contact?

5. Do you repeat back certain information to confirm that you understand?

6. Do you set up a follow-up meeting to provide what you've promised them at a later time?

How do you demonstrate to your employees that you're listening? The above questions will help you signal to them that you're actively involved in your conversations with them.

A friend of mine who currently operates her own management consulting firm shared with me the following story about a new manager. This manager spent a lot of time listening to his employees in the early stages of his new job, and it paid major dividends.

New managers obviously want to impress their boss and show them they are worthy of the promotion they have just received. So the smart thing is to dive into the work and get as much done as possible, right? No! You need to make an investment up front in knowing the team and finding out where the opportunities are to leverage talent. Are people living up to their potential? Are there hidden and unrecognized talents on the team?

I recall a young leader during my HR days who was moved to a failing branch that was in jeopardy of closing. I had visited a few months earlier and found the staff to be lethargic, uninterested, and performing poorly. We decided to make one last attempt by promoting him. (We'll call him Sam.)

Sam was in his early twenties and had so much enthusiasm, but he was also smart about people. Within a few months, the branch started to grow. Month after month, the numbers improved to a point where the branch was winning sales contests.

The interesting thing was that we didn't change the staff, only the manager. I visited a few months later, and it was a different place. The staff moved quickly and were happy and enthusiastic. Sam had discovered talents they didn't realize they had. They weren't what you would consider super performers, but Sam achieved extraordinary results from ordinary people. He listened to them and helped them discover their talents. He set goals with them, held them accountable, and recognized the small wins. He was genuinely interested in them, and they were loyal to him. He very quickly achieved greater success in his career, and he is currently a vice president in California.

New managers often just want to jump right in. They feel the need to do something and make a mark. Sometimes it's necessary to do that, but more often than not, this is the time to step back and listen. As Stephen Covey says in his groundbreaking book *The 7 Habits of Highly Effective People*, "Seek first to understand, then to be understood." We understand people by listening to them.

The Honest Conversation

While many managers struggle with positive recognition, many also struggle with acknowledging and managing poor performance. This may be one the most feared aspects of the manager's job: approaching a subordinate, peer, or boss to engage them in "the honest conversation." What is the honest conversation? It's a conversation to improve or change performance or to give performance-related news that won't likely garner a positive response. Those who have "no time" or whose strengths don't lie in problem solving or dealing with confrontation will often avoid this kind of conversation.

It's typically not enough to simply acknowledge someone's mistake; you need to use the honest conversation to encourage improvement or positive change. In my forty-two years of private, public, and not-for-profit sector experience, I have probably heard every excuse why managers don't have the honest conversation with their employees. Here is a brief sample:

- No time.
- I've got a job to do.
- They don't listen.
- It will make me look soft.
- I might as well do it myself.
- I am too busy.
- They don't understand.
- I don't like them.
- The union.
- They don't react very well.
- I don't know how.
- I don't know them.
- I'm not very good at it.
- It's not what I get paid to do.
- I don't want to hurt their feelings.

Avoiding these honest conversations can have a damaging effect on an organization. To prevent this and to encourage effective communication, a CEO friend of mine notes that managers need to look at these situations like "a fork-in-the-nose conversation." Imagine sticking the spines of a fork up a co-worker's nose and then leaning in to ask if you have their attention. The co-worker would undoubtedly say *yes*! The idea is that you need to ensure the other person understands the topic and the importance of the discussion. You first need to have their attention. This is the basis of effective communication.

Although the honest conversation may cause an employee pain (not from an actual fork, thankfully), avoiding the conversation can lead to more pain later on. Over the years, I have been called in on many consultations regarding terminations. In these cases, the manager has decided that an employee no longer fits or is not performing up to specifications (or a combinations of reasons). Ideally, when I meet with the manager, I hope to hear that there have been several performance coaching sessions with clearly defined expectations and productive follow-up meetings and that only after a period of documented discussions with the employee did the manager realize that termination was the best option. This would indicate that the manager has done every reasonable thing in a timely manner to try to facilitate positive change. Unfortunately, that is not often the case. Managers often don't conduct proper coaching sessions even though an employee's problematic behaviour has been going on for years.

In one case, I met with a manager who promoted an employee to supervisor only to realize within a matter of months that they had made a mistake. Instead of addressing the issue and potentially putting the person back in their previous position where they had been very successful, the manager allowed the substandard behaviour to continue. The supervisor was transferred to different jobs in different departments (also known as transferring the problem) until being returned to the original manager and department after eighteen years when no one else wanted to take responsibility. That's right. This employee was allowed to underperform for *eighteen years* because the manager was too afraid to have the honest conversation.

When I was called in to consult on the termination, the employee was only four years from becoming eligible to receive their full pension! If the manager had confronted the situation earlier, the employee probably would have been in a better place, and the company and the employees in this particular supervisor's charge wouldn't have suffered the incompetence and lack of supervisory guidance. In the end, the company terminated the supervisor's employment, and this person was devastated.

Each employee you communicate with can be categorized as follows:

- a star performer
- an average performer
- a poor performer

Although the poor performers will likely be only about 10 percent of your workforce, they tend to occupy most of your time because there is always a problem and always a complaint. Since poor performers do such lousy work, their projects are often incomplete or done to substandard levels. It will be either you or one of your high performers who end up picking up the slack.

If you avoid having the honest conversation with poor performers, two challenging situations will arise. First, other employees will see that you're not dealing with the problematic person, and they may think, "Why should I work so hard? They're paid the same money as I am, but they aren't held accountable for their substandard work. I might as well do the same." The risk here is that good performers can slip into becoming poor performers and then you'll have more of them to deal with. This phenomenon is what I call "the evil vortex of hell," and it can cause a lot of problems.

Second, someone still has to do the work assigned to the poor performer, so what do you do? You end up asking your star performers for help. Having your best employees pick up the slack essentially means penalizing them for being good at what they do. This can lead to star performers asking themselves whether there's a better place to work.

If you don't deal with a poor performer, the problem will perpetuate itself, usually resulting in a deteriorating work environment, losing good employees, decreasing productivity and quality, eroding customer service, and perhaps a decision by upper management to replace the manager—*you*. Below are a couple of helpful tools for dealing with this situation. The first is a set of questions to help you identify and deal with problems. The second is a quick reference for having the honest conversation with a poor performer.

Identifying and Dealing with Problems Regarding Poor Performance

- Have you categorized your employees by their performance record? Set up a grid and list employees in the appropriate area: star performer, average performer, or poor performer.

- Have you had the honest conversation with each employee in the poor performer group? If not, what's holding you back?

- Have you developed a performance/coaching plan for each poor performer? This should include identifying the problem, determining how the employee will correct the problem, establishing a time frame, and scheduling follow-up meetings.

- Do you also have a plan for each employee in the average performer group? Develop mentoring/coaching plans for your average performers to help them become star performers.

- Focus on the performance problem/behaviour, not the employee's personality: "Here's what I saw, and here's what I'd like to see."

- Ask for the employee's ideas and help in solving the problem: "What will you do differently next time? What did you learn?"

- Agree to and write down the next steps each of you will take: "What will you commit to? By when?"

- Express your confidence in the employee's ability to correct the problem and be sure to acknowledge any improvements: "I see you did it differently this time—good work!"

- Schedule follow-up meetings to assess and recognize progress and to have the honest conversation if there has been no improvement: "You have made excellent progress; it shows in your work" or "Your results haven't improved; we'll need to discuss this further."

Honest conversations, clear expectations, respectful recognition, and other communication techniques are important leadership tools. They have multiple effects, including fostering productivity, supporting relationships, creating and clarifying goals, and influencing others. If you want to help your employees attain their goals and achieve quantitative and qualitative success, you need to engage them on a meaningful level. We will go into more detail on poor, average, and star performers in Chapter 7.

Chapter 5

Engaging Your Crew: Building Trust and Respect

People often ask me why one team will perform well while another team will barely pass muster. Why do some teams respect and trust their leaders while others despise them and will only perform at the bare minimum? In recent years, the answer to this question has usually referred to employee engagement. If you have a highly engaged workforce, you will likely get good performance, which leads to greater productivity and increased customer satisfaction. Although there isn't one simple answer in all cases regarding employee engagement, we can at least point to missing factors as we dig into the root causes of low performance in teams. These factors are often related to trust and respect.

Employee Engagement

We've thus far covered a lot about the first steps you should take as a new manager. We've explored your goals, motivations, and characteristics as well as those of your employees. We've also covered the key aspects of workplace communication. Remember that we can define leadership as the ability to mobilize an individual or group towards a common goal. At its core, engagement allows you to navigate your interactions with others as you try to mobilize them. Specifically, high employee engagement has been credited with many positive outcomes, including

- higher productivity,
- improved customer service,
- employee retention, and
- employees speaking highly of the organization.

The ideas and concepts embedded in the theories regarding employee engagement are important for new managers to understand because an engaged workforce will get the results that managers need from their staff. Long-term business success is tied directly to customer service and productivity. Employee engagement is an important element in achieving high levels of both. A 2015 Gallup poll in the US revealed that about 32% of employees are engaged, 50.8% are not engaged, and 17.2% are actively disengaged.[1] This means that about one out of five employees could actually be doing damage to organizations.

Although the concept of engagement isn't new, the strategies associated with workplace engagement have

[1] Gallup, Inc. 2016. ªEmployee Engagement in U.S. Stagnant in 2015.º Gallup.com. January 13, 2016.
https://news.gallup.com/poll/188144/employee-engagement-stagnant-2015.aspx.

really come to prominence over the past fifteen years. These strategies have the same elements as those woven throughout this book: trust, communication, recognition, getting to know yourself and your employees, coaching, admitting when you're wrong, setting clear expectations, accountability, and executing.

By using and building on the suggestions in this book, you will have a better chance of building an engaged workforce and, in turn, an environment where employees are more likely to use their discretionary effort. Discretionary effort simply means going above and beyond regular duties. This includes the following:

- Staying late to finish a project
- Teaching another employee a better way to do things
- Asking for additional work
- Correcting another employee's mistake to prevent customer complaints

The idea is that your employees are doing something at their own discretion that was not assigned as part of their job. Just imagine how much you could improve your organization if you were able to increase the amount of discretionary effort your team was using. As we delve into engagement strategies, consider the following questions:

- On a scale of 1 to 10, with 1 being not very engaged and 10 being very engaged in building discretionary effort in your employees, how would you rate yourself on the engagement scale?

- On a scale of 1 to 10, with 1 being not very engaged and 10 being very engaged in contributing beyond their regular duties and job descriptions, how would you rate your employees on the engagement scale?

- What are some of the techniques you currently use to increase engagement (e.g., building trust, fostering mutual respect, providing support, listening, helping with decision-making, following up on promises, etc.)?

You may be limited in providing your employees with additional pay, bonuses, vacation time, or even development dollars, but you can you build engagement through leading the way by building trust, recognizing people's accomplishments, including people in decisions, supporting people when mistakes are made, and demonstrating integrity and honesty.

Engage Your Employees with Trust

Trust, in my view, encompasses several intimately intertwined leadership concepts, including honesty, integrity, and respect. When your employees trust you as a manager, they will be more likely to follow your instructions, directions, and advice without question or derision. Your employees may not always agree with you, but if they trust you, they will believe you're being honest and respectful with them. They will also be more apt to share important information with you. For instance, with a culture of trust, employees are more likely to report errors in a timely manner. This allows you to address errors before they can become more serious problems. This is just one reason trust is a cornerstone of great leadership. As this situation indicates, trust supports both engagement and larger organizational goals.

Early in my career, I had the opportunity to work for Bob Ruttan, a person I have considered my mentor, who was at the time the general manager of the Avondale Dairy division of Beatrice Foods Ltd. To this day, some forty-two years later, the lessons I learned from him continue to guide me in many of my leadership decisions.

I became a shipping and warehouse supervisor when I was about twenty-three years old. One of my responsibilities was to order dairy products we didn't produce but our stores and home delivery people needed. In one instance, I had placed orders for a yogurt product promotion based on what our salespeople believed we needed. After the two-week promotion, we had to throw out approximately $7,000 worth of product because of expiry dates. Now this wasn't entirely my fault because I had received my instructions from the sales team. What I could have done, however, was give the sales team up-to-date daily numbers so they could react more quickly to the fact that the product wasn't selling fast enough. (Bear in mind that this was before electronic tracking of daily sales.)

To complicate matters, my boss had to report the loss to the president of the dairy division. I still remember looking over and seeing him with his fingers dug into the arms of his black leather chair, realizing he was about to get severally reprimanded for mistakes I had made. However, he simply and calmly said to me, "We just dumped $7,000 worth of product…so what did you learn from that?"

My boss wasn't looking to fix blame for my error. He trusted me to come up with a solution to prevent it from happening again—and it didn't. He trusted me, and I trusted him to treat me with the understanding I needed, especially when I was young and learning that I was a leader. He also taught me the importance of celebrating mistakes. He told me, "If you're not making mistakes once in a while, you're probably not trying anything new; if you're not trying anything new, you're maintaining the status quo." The operative concept here is taking calculated risks. A culture of trust allows engaged employees to take risks that are well thought out and have an anticipated chance of success.

Another thing about Bob that stands out in my mind is the simplicity of his approach to management. Remember that this was the late seventies and early eighties; leadership development was only just starting to gain mainstream popularity. "Management training" was still the term people used, and I remember a conversation we had about managing people. He was a

Rotarian, and he said that he used the Rotary Four-Way Test to guide his actions when dealing with people:

1. Is it the truth?
2. Is it fair to all concerned?
3. Will it build goodwill and better friendships?
4. Will it be beneficial to all concerned?

I have never forgotten these principles. When dealing with problems and employee issues, I have often thought how Bob would approach them. These simple principles have served me well in issues of trust and fairness. Building trust requires getting to know people on a deeper level, beyond their employee status or level of productivity. In the seventies, employees were expected to keep work at work and leave home at home. I think it's short-sighted at best to believe this separation can actually exist in today's workforce. There are just too many things that blur the boundaries between work and home (e.g., dual-income families, telecommuting, smartphones, nonstandard work schedules, etc.). And let's not forget that your own development as an employee encompasses aspects of both your work and home life.

Management by wandering around (MBWA) is a leadership concept advocated by Tom Peters and Robert H. Waterman, Jr., the authors of the international bestselling book *In Search Of Excellence*. It can help you not only transition from an individual contributor to a manager but also establish trust with your employees. MBWA simply means getting up from your desk and walking around to interact with your customers and employees. Doing so might actually teach you something about the way you could be or should be running your business.

I started to practice this concept after hearing about it in the eighties, and I still use it today. As I talk to people on these informal walkabouts, I find out amazing things about them, their jobs, and the organization. Showing an interest in people can often assist you in building trust, making decisions, and knowing where to focus your attention. The following story illustrates the importance of talking to people.

In the early nineties, I consulted with an organization that needed me to figure out why they were having so many problems. It was regarding a manufacturing plant that made conveyor belting for industrial use that wasn't performing well in many of the important metrics that would ensure its long-term viability. The problems included low employee satisfaction, poor product quality, low productivity compared to other plants in the company, and high absentee rates. There was, however, one exception: the shipping and receiving department. It had the highest productivity (number of products shipped per employee), the highest quality standards (errors per hundred items shipped), the lowest absentee rates, and the highest employee satisfaction scores as reported through the company's employee satisfaction survey. Interestingly, the average age of the employees in the department was forty-six years old, but their supervisor was only twenty-six. I figured this was a good place to start, so I met with this young man to figure out what was going on, or rather what was going right.

When I met Phil, he was quite different from what I had expected. He was quiet, reflective, wasn't egotistical or self-centered, and had admitted he had no post-secondary education or specific managerial training. In other words, he wasn't a professional manager. He was just a young man who started as a part-time shipper when he was sixteen. He started working full-time after completing high school and accepted a supervisor position at the ripe age of twenty-three.

I asked him what his secret to success was, hoping to learn about some brilliant new management technique he had discovered. After what appeared to be some deliberation, he took a few puffs on his cigarette and said, "I talk to people." That's it. He went on to explain how he made the effort to chat with people every day about their families and any special interests he had come to learn about. For example, he knew that one of his crew coached minor hockey and that the team's practices occurred on Friday mornings at 5 a.m. This was why he would always arrive at work thirty minutes late that day of the week. Phil made allowances for this. Another employee liked to go hunting in the fall, so Phil would make sure to give him time off for his annual trip. It wasn't that he was giving these employees special privileges. He simply understood what was important to them and figured out how to accommodate them without negatively affecting the department. As a result, his crew trusted him and respected him and responded with increased engagement and increased productivity.

In my conversations with Phil, I learned several key things about establishing trust. Based on our discussions and my own observations, I identified five critical factors for his leadership success:

1. *Be curious.* Be genuinely interested in people. Ask questions to find out more about them. Phil took an interest in people and made them feel like they mattered.

2. *Find and support passion.* Find out what people are passionate about. Many managers complain that they can't connect with certain people. They need to find some common ground or at least understand their employee's passions. Phil made sure that his staff had the opportunity to spend time doing these things outside of work.

3. *Eliminate preconceived notions.* Don't rely solely on the assessments or opinions of others. Phil didn't rely on preconceived notions or what other people had said about his staff. He didn't completely discount them, but by talking to his people and getting to know them, he was able to formulate his own opinions.

4. *Share personal information.* When Phil shared his own passions with his staff, it had a tremendous impact on building trust. Sharing personal information builds reciprocity. I call it chipping off little pieces of yourself to share with others. Do this and people will share little pieces of themselves with you.

5. *Make people feel like they matter.* Through recognition, trust, and engagement, employees will feel like they matter to you and the organization. This will have a positive effect. If you continually acknowledge that you value people and their work, it will help maintain trust.

As a new manager, try these tips to cultivate and maintain trust and engagement with your employees:

- Demonstrate a genuine interest in people.

- Get to know what motivates each team member.

- Spend meaningful time with people.

- Participate in employee events.

- Know every employee by name.

- Be willing to help.

- Have lunch or coffee with people.

- Acknowledge the value of people's contributions.

Trust Is Difficult to Gain but Easy to Lose

Trust is important. A lack of trust can have far-reaching negative effects. It's even worse if you break someone's trust. If that happens, everyone in the organization will know about it. Trust is difficult to gain, easy to lose, and almost impossible to regain. For instance, I remember a bad situation regarding a fairly senior employee in an organization I consulted with. She had lost the trust of her peers, subordinates, and superiors as a result of a series of events in which she lied to and misled people. She was left without anyone to support any of her initiatives. The problem for the organization was that some of the initiatives would have had positive results, but they were rejected because of the employees' absolute distrust of this leader. After several years (yes, *years*), her employment was terminated, but the damage had been done. The organization had suffered, and the woman's career was completely destroyed.

Given that building trust is a key competency for leaders, let's look at how it's done. You can demonstrate trustworthiness through your actions, but many leaders build reputations around the idea that they never make mistakes. It's more reasonable to assume, however, that they simply never admit to making mistakes or that they find ways to blame others. Politicians are particularly good at this sleight of hand. In some circles, admitting to mistakes is considered a sign of weakness, while in other circles it's considered a mark of integrity and accountability.

Many people don't realize that mistakes can offer opportunities to reinforce trust. When you make a mistake as a manager, you may be tempted to

- continue going in the wrong direction so you don't have to admit the mistake,

- blame something or someone else for the error and then change your course of action, or

- say nothing and simply change the course of action (i.e., "It's none of your business why we're changing; just do your job").

I challenge you to follow a different path. Trust that people will respect you for being honest enough to admit to your mistake and for being responsible enough to take the appropriate actions to fix it. You might say something like, "We need to change direction on this problem because I made a mistake. After talking to several people, I think this is a better direction to go." Some people will try to use this admission against you, but in my experience, most people will be supportive of you when you demonstrate honesty and integrity. Admitting to a mistake demonstrates vulnerability, which reinforces trust. This strengthens your relationships, which in turn reinforces employee engagement.

During my travels a few years ago, I met a management consultant who specialized in financial services. He shared a story about a manager he encountered during a facilitation session he was having with employees of a financial institution:

> I find in my travels as a leadership consultant that when there's problem in the team, there is most often a lack of trust. There's often a lack of trust between team members, but ultimately there's also a lack of trust in the manager because they're not managing the situation.
>
> New leaders often struggle with this because they want to build relationships with their new team and often hesitate to deal with the issues for fear of damaging their relationships. I have found that we don't really "manage people"; we manage ourselves, and as we move into manager roles, it's learning new behaviours that will support the kind of manager we want to be. We cannot control others, but we can influence them. So it's our own behaviours that we must change in order to influence change in the team.
>
> I recall a time when I was facilitating a group of new frontline managers who were responsible for unionized staff. There was a gentleman in the back of the room who made it

clear he didn't want to be there. He argued every point and made it clear he wasn't changing anything. What I found interesting was that he was quite vocal about the nasty, lazy, unchanging people he was forced to have on his team. In his mind, there was nothing he could do.

When I asked him how he was managing the situation, he described his behaviour, which was, in my estimate, nasty and unchanging. He was a victim of his circumstances and didn't believe anything he might do would make a difference. He most likely supported the system the previous boss set (or maybe the one set by the boss before that). The system was so strongly set that a change in his behaviour would probably come as a shock, but over time he could likely build trust and change the culture of that team.

What I would have liked to see him do is just listen to what his team was saying—really hear them and let them know he values them. This doesn't mean he has to put up with substandard work. It's how he reacts and manages himself that will change their behaviours. Unfortunately, I don't believe he will look within himself to make these changes, and either he will be a very frustrated manager with an unhappy team or he may not be successful as a manager and will have to make other career choices.

This story is sad because it's a situation the manager could have fixed if he only looked within himself and admitted that he was responsible for the demoralized staff. It takes courage for managers to admit to being wrong and to change the way they do things. People feel vulnerable when they reveal their shortcomings and ask for help. It's funny to me that even today we actually believe we always have to be right and can never make a mistake or ask for help. Is it arrogance that makes us believe we should be smarter than all the people who report to us? The best approach for leaders is to engage those closest to the work rather than disengage or alienate them. You need to build trust among your staff if you want to become the best leader you can be.

Chapter 6

Doing Safety Drills: Role Clarity

The safety drills that passengers have to go through before the cruise ship leaves the harbour amazed me the first time I took a cruise, but I grew bored of them by the third or fourth time. Upon reflection, however, I think that understanding your role and the roles of your crew isn't something you want to start figuring out as your ship sinks in the middle of the North Atlantic on a frigid winter night.

Role clarity is one of the most critical aspects of good management. It helps form the basis of accountability in high-performing teams. It basically means that everyone knows what their job is, what they're trying to accomplish, and what they're accountable for. When you're an individual contributor, you need to understand your goals and how they relate to the goals of the organization. When you become a manager, however, you need to understand your goals and how they relate to the goals of the organization *and* your employees.

It's time to examine your leadership style and understand what you can do in your role as manager to influence your employees in their own roles.

What's Your Leadership Style?

Although it's important that employees under your charge understand what their role is, it's just as important that you know what your role is as you lead people. What's your leadership style? Well, what *is* a leadership style? At its root, it's simply how you lead people. How you lead is largely determined by your strengths and competencies, your personal traits, your value system, and your situational experiences.

There are many tests you can take to identify your management and leadership style, and there is plenty of literature outlining the strengths and competencies that make great managers and leaders. Over the past several years, however, we've moved away from the practice of identifying deficiencies and weaknesses and finding ways to fix them. Instead, we now have powerful tools for identifying and improving important strengths. Gallup and Zenger Folkman are two companies that have developed such tools. The idea is that if people don't really change much over their working lifetimes, it's a waste of time to try to change weaknesses into strengths. It's much more effective to build existing strengths into great strengths.

It's also important to understand how your personal traits and your value system affect your leadership style. Your personal traits are the various qualities you express as a person. Your character is the sum of those traits. Depending on your value system, the more you display your strengths and traits, the more people will respect your character and trust you. The leadership skills you develop as a new manager depend on your character. Identifying your traits and values will help you understand the larger systems that guide your choices and influence the development of your strengths. Understanding all of this will lead to better results on your personal and professional journey toward success.

Let's look at some key concepts more closely. By understanding the differences between beliefs, values, skills, and traits, you'll better understand yourself and others.

- *Beliefs.* These are deeply rooted assumptions or convictions you have about people, places, concepts, or things. You have beliefs about life, death, right, wrong, culture, nature, and so on. You might have certain beliefs about certain cultures. You might think some are industrious while others are lazy.

  Beliefs can positively and negatively influence how you treat certain groups. If people from different cultures belong to your team, how will you ensure you will treat them fairly?

- *Values.* These are your attitudes about the worth of people, places, concepts, or things. Your values influence your choices and your behaviour. For example, you might value family more than privacy or money more than friendship.

  Values are incredibly difficult to change. Let's say an employee with young children wants to spend as much time as possible outside of regular work hours attending family events and their children's activities. Let's also say another employee wants to work as much overtime as possible and will take on every work assignment thrown at them. Does this mean one employee is more committed to the job than the other? Not necessarily. These employees might have different value systems, but they could be equally productive at work. You need to understand how your own value system affects the people who work with you.

- *Skills.* These are the knowledge and abilities you acquire in life. The ability to learn a new skill varies with each individual. Analytical, communication, customer service, organizational, problem solving, and teamwork skills are among the many useful skills in the workplace.

  Skills are easier to change compared to beliefs and values. We usually learn our beliefs and values over a long period, often through family, school, and religious organizations, for example, and they become embedded in us. However, we can learn new skills and update current skills throughout our lives. You should constantly assess and grow your skills as part of your career development.

- *Traits.* These are your distinguishing qualities and characteristics. Your character or personality is the sum of your personal traits. After much research in this area, theorists have identified numerous personality traits. These include introversion, extroversion, adaptability, creativity, defensiveness, honesty, objectivity, persistence, and self-control.

  Many consider traits as those habitual patterns of thought and emotions that remain stable over time. It's important for you to be aware of your own traits so you know how they inform your character, which in large part is how people view you as a person and a leader.

As you consider how these elements influence your leadership style, you should also consider other factors such as your work environment. For example, do you work for a highly autocratic organization? Is it hierarchal and driven only by profit? How will these factors also influence your leadership style? What is your boss' leadership style? Is she collaborative? Does she expect all employees to have a voice in the decisions?

All of these factors matter. You have to figure out how they will affect your personal leadership style. Will you bend to the demands of your superiors or will you find your own style and lead that way at all costs? It will sometimes depend on where you are in your career. If you're at the beginning or end, you might decide to bend to the will of your bosses to avoid rocking the boat too much. However, if you're at a point where you have flexibility and multiple job opportunities, you might decide to work for an organization that shares your values and will allow for the growth of your leadership style.

What's for certain is that you have control over how you want to lead people. You can't necessarily control how the company is led or managed (unless you're the CEO), but you can determine how to lead the people in your department in a positive way even if certain forces external to you manage things in not so positive ways. If you can't, then perhaps you'll have to decide whether to leave the organization. If you're going to spend thirty years working five days a week, which amounts to more than seven thousand days of your productive years, shouldn't you be doing something you love (or at least like)? I realize that we sometimes have to sacrifice some of our autonomy (when we're starting out, for example), but we shouldn't have to do this our entire working life. If at all possible, don't you want to be great at what you do?

The path to becoming a great leader starts from knowing who you are and what you do well. We will now look at how you can get started on the journey to greatness.

What Is Your Primary Leadership Style?

Are you a manager who collaborates or are you autocratic? Do you demonstrate more servant leadership traits or would you consider yourself more of a situational leader?

Servant leadership is a philosophy that's been around for ages, but Robert K. Greenleaf coined the term and popularized the concept in his essay entitled "The Servant As Leader," first published in 1970. Greenleaf turns the traditional model of leadership upside down. Whereas in the traditional model, the employees serve the leader, in the servant model, the leader is there to serve the employees. This shift is a shared leadership model that provides the opportunity for employees to contribute to the organization differently by allowing them to take part more fully. Greenleaf expresses a duty of care that the leader has for their employees and identifies developing people one of the main priorities.

Situational leadership theory is a model Paul Hersey developed in his book *The Situational Leader.* Hersey takes the position that individuals' leadership style depends on each situation they face. He suggests that having one leadership style is like having only one tool in your toolbox, a hammer for example, and so you start treating everything as though there's only one possible approach. If all you have is a hammer, everything looks like a nail. Hersey identified four leadership styles that a leader can use depending on the situation: delegating, participating, selling, and telling.

Here are a few questions to get you thinking about your own leadership style:

1. What traits have you exhibited as an individual contributor will influence your leadership style?

2. What leadership style is right for the situation or culture of your organization?

3. What leadership styles are you uncomfortable with? How will this affect your career as a manager?

4. What are the leadership styles of some of the great leaders you have heard about, read about, or observed?

Remember that your leadership style will evolve over time depending on your experiences, but it is very much a part of who you are. Below is a table I have put together outlining common leadership styles that have been written about over the past forty years. This is by no means an exhaustive list. My intent is to present a sample based on my experience. Use this information to identify your primary leadership style. This is the style you tend to use when you deal with a crisis or are under extreme pressure.

Style	Description	Characteristics
Dictator*	• Direction and control from the top • Autocratic/authoritarian	• Kicks ass, takes names, and doesn't take any prisoners • Strict, close control over people through the close regulation of policies and procedures • Sets goals individually and engages primarily in one-way and downward communication • Controls discussions and dominates interactions • Possibly uses fear as a motivator*
Collaborator	• Shares in the decision-making • Treats all team members with equality	• Seeks understanding and has strong interpersonal skills • Values opinions and sees conflict as a way to get to a better solution • Looks for lots of ideas and information to help inform their decisions (but not to the point of procrastination)
Social Director	• Makes decisions that foster agreement • Brings differing ideas together • Avoids confrontation and conflict	• Provides people with all the equipment and tools required to complete the work • Avoids interfering with decisions, sometimes viewed as an absent manager/leader • Avoids conflict, sometimes agreeing with several differing opinions just to maintain what they consider to be harmony • Creates the "organizational lovefest"
Harmonizer	• Allows people complete freedom to make decisions • Promotes the interests of the group.	• Consensus, agreement, harmony, compromise, accord • Grants permission and provides support at an emotional level • Provides an understanding shoulder to lean on in professional and personal situations
Influencer/Manipulator	• Formulates ideas or directions in advance • Demonstrates visionary or "ahead of the pack" thinking	• Manipulates or maneuvers people in a certain direction by making promises or threats • Tells people their idea and then asks them for their opinion
Traditional	• Focuses on motivating people through a system of rewards and punishments • Respects and follows hierarchies	• Maturity, goal-setting, increasing efficiency, increasing productivity
Developer	• Changes or transforms the organization by tapping into the potential of the employees	• Uses people's ability to think about what's next • Uses questions such as "What if?" "Why?" "How might this change?" and "What did you learn from this?"

* Remember that there is no such thing as bad leadership. At its extreme, the dictator style is not a leadership style but an abuse of power.

A great deal of the writing on management has focused on the idea of managing based on your strengths and the context of the situation. Some of the more popular titles, including The *Situational Leader* by Paul Hersey and *The Managerial Grid* by Robert R. Blake and Jane Mouton, suggest that great leaders are more mobile or successful when they use and adapt different styles to suit different situations. For example, your leadership may take on more of a dictator style during times of crisis and more of a harmony style during times of extreme calm and stability. Although you may see yourself leading in different ways depending on the situation, I suggest focusing on your primary style. Think of a time when you were in a crisis situation in your professional or personal life. What traits did you exhibit and what strengths did you draw on?

It has become evident to me is that it's impossible to lead without "displaying high integrity and honesty," regardless of what style you predominately lead from. This is a concept that John H. Zenger and Joseph R. Folkman explore in their book *The Extraordinary Leader.* In summary, they say that people aren't likely to follow someone who doesn't demonstrate a certain level of character, and there is no leadership without any followers. We saw this with certain leaders such as former Ontario premier Dalton McGuinty and former U.S. secretary of state and presidential candidate Hillary Clinton, who ultimately struggled as leaders when people started to perceive them as lacking honesty and integrity as politicians.

Why is it important to know your leadership style? For me, it's really simple: If you understand your style, you can build on it, strengthen it, and adapt it when necessary. It's no different from understanding your strengths in other aspects. If you're a great pastry chef, you probably don't spend a lot of time perfecting your sauce recipes. Likewise, if you're great at preparing budgets and designing buildings, you may not be the strongest at engaging and inspiring employees.

As you navigate your managerial role, you will be more likely to reach your personal and professional goals if you identify and build on your strengths. As a bonus, you will also be more likely to understand the strengths and skills of others, which will allow you to properly use the human resources at your disposal for achieving your goals. If you keep aware of what you can control, such as how to use people's strengths, you will be better able to steer your ship toward success.

The Importance of Role Clarity

At the beginning of this chapter, I talked about the importance of passengers and crew knowing their roles on a cruise ship in the event of an emergency. Without this preparation, there would be mass confusion and chaos in a critical situation, which could lead to lost lives. It may come as a surprise to you that some industries operate daily with constant concerns about role clarity that could be placing others at great risk. Consider the significance of role clarity when it comes to nuclear power generation, water treatment, petrochemical refinement, pharmaceutical production, and chemical processing.

If there is any doubt of the importance of role clarity, one only has to turn to the Lac-Mégantic rail disaster that occurred in the Eastern Townships of Quebec in 2013, when an unattended freight train derailed in the downtown area, resulting in a fire and the explosion of multiple tank cars. This caused forty-seven deaths and the destruction of nearly half of the downtown area. Although three railway employees were acquitted in January 2018 of charges including criminal negligence causing death, a case remains in the courts involving railway executives, as the Crown is pursuing the argument that procedures were either not in place or not followed regarding the setting of brakes on unattended rail cars.

But a lack of role clarity doesn't always result in major disaster. It can also lead to jobs not being completed on time, poor quality control results, equipment damage, and poor customer service. One thing is for certain: A lack of role clarity can have a negative impact on productivity and performance. It's your job as a manager to make sure that employees understand their role and are adequately trained to perform their role properly. This sometimes requires practice and retraining as critical aspects of the role change or are upgraded.

Role clarity also affects employees who provide services. Consider, for example, firefighters, teachers, and nurses. People need to know what role these professionals play in their safety and the safety of their families. People also need to know who to contact when they need assistance, whether it's an emergency or to deal with personal issues.

Alignment

I often refer to alignment as being like singing from the same song sheet. Your alignment is the degree to which you know how your job fits into the organization's common purpose. This relates to that story of the janitor at NASA whose job was simply to clean and maintain his work area. He knew that the work he did was ultimately connected to the final stage of putting a man on the moon. His work was a small but integral part of that mission, and every other person working at NASA at the time, regardless of what they did, also played a role in it. Everybody worked in harmony to achieve this single goal.

When you consider your own leadership style, try to determine whether it aligns with the organization. If your management style contradicts the organization's culture, it will be like trying to push string up a hill. As we've discussed, there may be times when your personal values or beliefs come into conflict with what the organization does. For example, if you've been offered a position as sales manager of a large tobacco company but a family member of yours recently passed away from lung cancer after years of smoking, you may have a hard time making and maintaining a commitment to the company's goals. This is because your values or beliefs might never be in alignment with the organization.

This is an obvious example, but it does illustrate how alignment can be critical to your success. You might be prepared to sacrifice some of your personal beliefs and values early in your career just to get your foot in the door, but it will be difficult to contradict what's important to you over the long haul.

It will also be difficult for your employees to grasp the magnitude of their contributions if they don't fully understand what you do, what the organization does, and what their role is. The following questions will help you close any gaps.

1. Do your employees understand what your leadership style and role is?
2. Do your employees understand their roles? Are they adequately trained to maximize their contributions?
3. Do your employees understand the bigger organizational goal? Do they know how they contribute to it?

In my role as head of human resources at Brock University, I occasionally get a chance to participate in new employee orientation sessions. All new employees in every job category attend these sessions, including those with jobs in faculty, information technology, finance, human resources, legal, and maintenance—in other words, everybody who joins as a full-time employee.

It can be fairly easy to connect the dots of why new

members of the faculty are there. However, some of the other positions can be fairly far removed from the core research and teaching that goes on at the university. Regardless, I try to use these orientation sessions to discuss the contributions that everyone makes to help students cross the stage and graduate. I also outline how everyone's work contributes to the research efforts of the professors at the university. It's my small effort to create alignment with the bigger picture. I also talk about what I do and how human resources contribute to the bigger picture.

I was working with the support staff of one of our law enforcement agencies a few years ago and was interviewing people from the compensation team. My first question to each of them was "So what do you do?" What I heard in response has stuck with me as a defining moment. The answer from every single person was some version of this: "My job is to make sure the officers get paid and get their benefits so they don't have to worry about those things and can focus their attention on keeping people safe." I was floored. I had never heard this type of alignment and pride in my life. This taught me that it can be accomplished and that employees, regardless of their role, can understand the bigger picture of the organization they work for.

Section 3

Out at Sea: Dealing with Uncertainties and Inevitabilities

"Never give in, never give in, never, never, never…."
—Winston Churchill

Your first day as a manager has drawn to a close. You climb down from the quarterdeck. Your face has been battered by the wind, your clothes are soaked from the sea mist, and your legs are shaky from standing on an unsteady deck all day, but you feel good that the day is over and you didn't get swept overboard. You return to the captain's cabin with glazed eyes and your head filled with so much information it seeps out your ears. You begin to think about tomorrow, which is a brand new day.

It's time to synthesize what you've learned with what you already know. So far, you've learned that you can control many aspects of your life, including your perceptions, relationships, and career experiences. Although the tides of your career (and your daily work) may shift, the fundamentals of management and leadership can remain a guiding star in rocky seas. In this section, you will start to get the feeling of what it's like to be alone on the bridge. Management can be a lonely place, especially when problems arise or when decisions need to be made. This is when you start to put some experience into action and test your assumptions and skills. In a sense, this is where you earn your stripes.

Although how we value certain contributions may change, one thing remains consistent: the value organizations put on a manager's ability to get stuff done. What has changed is how North American businesses get stuff done with fewer bridges burned. Organizations today prefer to accomplish things respectfully to avoid having employees leave and possibly broadcast on social media what a lousy organization they worked for. This kind of publicity is now fairly common, and it can have a far-reaching negative impact on a company's reputation and future labour pool.

Managing employees with respect encourages becoming engaged instead of simply trying to survive in various levels of meritocracy. Certainly in North America, the command and control mentality of the past has a much-reduced impact today because people, especially the good people, now have less tolerance for autocratic organizations and more opportunities and mobility to choose kinder and more collaborative organizations to work for.

Chapter 7

Alone on the Bridge: Mastering Accountability

A position of leadership can be a very lonely place. You're sometimes expected to make unpopular decisions regarding your staff, and at other times you might be at odds with your superiors for not agreeing with their decisions. As Gordon B. Hinckley once said in a speech, "The price of leadership is loneliness. The price of adherence to conscience is loneliness. The price of adherence to principle is loneliness." This is the world that leaders, especially the good ones, live in. Many people have the ability to say yes all the time, but leaders have to be able to say no and make unpopular decisions.

I'm reminded of a situation that happened early in my career when I was at Avondale Dairy. My boss came to me with an idea about how we loaded our trucks. He had this idea about moving away from loading our trucks with individually stacked crates of milk products. To give you an idea of what this was like, plastic milk cases full of dairy products were stacked about five cases high and weighed about 225 pounds. We moved them by dragging them along the floor using a long metal hook with a handle. His suggestion was to load the products directly onto wooden skids or pallets and then move them onto the trucks in bulk with forklifts. I bucked the idea because I didn't feel we were properly set up to assemble the pallets and felt it would be time-consuming and cumbersome. Also, I was pretty confident that this idea and the additional work would piss off my warehouse staff. Deep down, I knew this was the future of how we needed to handle product shipping, but I just didn't feel we were ready for it. My boss made it quite simple for me, however. He said, "Look, I'm going on holidays for two weeks, and when I return, I want the product to be on skids." Message received!

So I got to thinking about how to get this started and how to sell it to the warehouse crew. I could have played the same game of just telling them to do it, but I thought it might be better to explain why and how this might work. In other words, I learned my first true lesson of loneliness. Everyone was upset about the change, and questions like "Why do we need to change?" and "Whose dumb idea was this?" occupied much of the discussion. I decided before the discussion that I wouldn't place the blame on anyone. I instead had the staff focus on how it was going to be the future and that we might as well start now.

I told them we would start the following week. I made arrangements to bring in additional part-time help to assist with building the pallets until we could come up with a better setup, but a lot of the warehouse staff remained distant and wary of me for some time. I had entered a new phase in my own growth and understanding as a manager and leader—that of having to make unpopular but necessary decisions for the business. In hindsight, it was the right decision, but there were several days when it was very frosty in the warehouse (and I'm not referring to the weather).

The old expression "the buck stops here" is often a philosophy of the frontline manager. Sure, you can try to push the blame up the line, but you won't gain much respect from either your staff or your superiors. It's unavoidable; the relationships you have with your subordinates are bound to change as a result of some of the decisions you'll have to make, but it's not always for the worse. You can sometimes earn a lot of respect by making a decision even though it still makes you feel very lonely.

The Voice of Doubt

Throughout my career, I've heard people talk about both the fear of failure and the fear of success. The reasons for having a fear of failure seem obvious (at least to me). Most of us don't want to fail at a job or task, and we certainly don't want to be tagged with the title of "a failure" in life. Most of us seem to have a pretty good idea of how we can be successful. This might include getting a good education, gathering knowledge in an area of expertise, networking to increase contacts and develop future employment opportunities, working hard, treating people with respect, etc. The reasons for having a fear of success, however, seem less obvious. After all, who would be afraid of success? Isn't it something we all want? Career success can bring more opportunities, money, prestige, and power. Regardless, the fear of success is more prevalent than many realize.

For the purposes of our discussion here, I have named this phenomenon the voice of doubt. The voice of doubt can present itself in many ways, including fear or a lack of self-confidence. How will you handle your new job? What if you make a mistake? Will people respect you? In contrast, it can also manifest itself as overconfidence or cockiness, where you might trust your own opinions too much or undervalue the opinions of others.

As you start to look at who you are as a leader, it's important to identify anything that could be holding you back. You can identify triggers or characteristics through self-reflection, 360° feedback surveys, or professional coaching. It's not within the scope of this book to help you uncover your personal saboteur, but as you develop yourself, consider what influences your values, decisions, and actions. Remember that your voice of doubt isn't you; it's destructive chatter that you need to separate from yourself. Also keep in mind that your employees deal with their own voice of doubt.

The following story is about a young woman I had the pleasure to work with several years ago. In my opinion, Kristen had all the characteristics required to be a great leader. One day, she was presented with an opportunity to move to the next level. Did she take the opportunity or was she be held back by fear and her concerns regarding her ability to be successful?

Kristen graduated from university in 2008, but she couldn't find work directly in her field, which was environmental science, and she had started to lose interest in her course of study. In her second year of university, however, she had landed a job as a teller with a financial institution. She was able to work Friday and Saturday nights through the school year and full-time through the summer. As a result, she was able to graduate debt-free, which was not something many of her friends were able to manage unless their parents had higher incomes than most of their middle-class peers.

Kristen was able to turn this job into a full-time gig after graduation. She then moved into a financial services assistant position. In the fourth year of her employment, she got the opportunity to fill in as a part-time Saturday supervisor when the full-time supervisor went on a three-week vacation to Europe. The feedback from her supervisor upon on her return and from the branch manager was that she was going places. She was good with people and understood the business. Although this was a small organization and there probably wasn't going to be an opportunity for a promotion for at least three years, they would offer her opportunities when people went on vacation and she would get an opportunity for a full-time management position within that time frame if things went well.

The problem for Kristen was that she didn't want to wait that long and deal with the uncertainty. She really liked the role of supervisor and didn't like this process of going back and forth. She liked the organization and the people she worked with, but she also recognized the limitations a small company offered, such as little room for promotions, development, and personal growth and few opportunities to make more money and work in different locations.

The other issue playing on Kristen's mind was the fact that one of her friends had landed a job at one of the major financial institutions in Canada. This friend had also set Kristen up with a meeting with her boss. He was eager to recruit young, motivated people with some real experience into his branch network. If the meeting went well, it would mean lots of opportunities for advancement, the opportunity to work in different major Canadian cities, the possibly of international travel, lots of training and development, and definitely more money.

But Kristen was reluctant. What was the problem? What was holding her back? She confided in me some of the major issues. First, the organization she worked for was the only place she had ever worked. It was small, and she knew everyone. She was basically going for an interview for one of the largest financial institutions in the country. In fact, it was one of the largest and most successful in the world. Maybe she would turn out to be a fraud. Maybe she didn't know what she was doing. Maybe they would figure it out and would fire her and unceremoniously usher her out of her new job within the first month. (Thoughts like these add up to a pattern known as "impostor syndrome.") She also didn't know anyone. How would she learn about the organization? Who would be there to show her the ropes? What if her potential boss asked her what she wanted to accomplish in the future and she didn't have the right answer? Maybe she would make her friend look bad for setting up the interview. The thoughts seemed overwhelming to her. Maybe she should just stay put and wait for a few years….

The issues behind the voice of doubt are too complex to address completely in the context of this book, but most leaders face them at some time in their careers. This self-doubt, indecisiveness, and lack of confidence can undermine our ability to succeed and sometimes prove to be a self-fulfilling prophecy. This voice of doubt can sabotage our success.

It's amazing how powerful our inner voice can be when it carries negative messages and how we often ignore it or don't believe it when it carries positive messages. In my own career and through my independent coaching and consulting practice, I have had to find ways to address certain issues of self-doubt for both my clients and myself, and I have found the following questions to be a great help in providing insight:

1. What's holding me back?
2. What am I afraid of?
3. What's the worst that can happen if I'm wrong?
4. Can I live with the worst possible outcome?
5. Am I at least 51% sure this will work? If yes,

can I make the decision and figure out the other stuff as I go?

When I start this line of questioning with people, they often ask me why I'm asking these questions. Many admit that it's sometimes easier to ignore the problem than confront it head on. What they often find after some exploration using these questions is that the problem isn't as big as they thought it was.

I recall a situation I had with a client a few years ago that surprised me. We talked quite a bit about his fear of failure during a certain work-related activity. We talked about how his being afraid of failure was a fairly normal thing that happens to people early in their careers. As our talk continued, I was surprised to find out that he had had some successes already in his career and a few failures. I asked how he felt when he had these successes, and he said "stressed out." When I asked how he felt when he had failures, he said "relieved."

When I asked why he felt that way, he said that the expectations from his superiors seemed to increase every time he was successful and that failures seemed to normalize things for him. He said that he could probably have avoided the failures but instead somehow sabotaged things so he wouldn't succeed. These were, for the most part, fairly minor things such as not getting a report done by a certain date or not following up on an important customer complaint. Nonetheless, he viewed them a serious failures.

We continued our discussions over several weeks. We talked about what success meant and what failure meant and what he personally wanted to build. After a couple of months, he came to the conclusion that what he wanted to build wasn't compatible with the failures he had orchestrated and that there was no reason for him to fear success. He decided he should embrace and celebrate successes, as they contributed to his life goals and professional goals.

The 10/80/10 Factor of Management

I can't remember where I first heard of the 10/80/10 rule, but people apply it to many concepts, both inside and outside of business. As much as I would like to say that everyone who works for you will be a great employee, the truth is that some will be and some won't be. The percentages for each group shown below, although simplistic, reflect the employee performance distribution in many organizations:

Star Performer	10 percent
Average Performer	80 percent
Poor Performer	10 percent

It's unlikely that many companies have this exact distribution, but most likely have employees in each of these categories. As a manager, you need to think about how you will manage each of these groups and, above all, not forget that some groups require more attention than others and most likely different strategies. It would be dangerous to assume that you don't have employees in each of these categories because it could mean overlooking a problem or failing to provide development opportunities or proper recognition, which could result in poorly performing employees staying and/or high performers (or those with potential) leaving. So what group does each of your employees fall into?

- *Star performer*. About 10 percent of your employees may be star performers. These are employees who need very little direction. They will often come to you with a solution far in advance of any apparent problem. You call upon them in times of crisis, and they never let you down. When managing these employees, the best leadership technique is often to just stay out of their way.

- *Average performer.* About 80 percent of your employees may fall into this category. These are the "Steady Eddies" and "Steady Bettys" who show up every day and do good work. You manage them by giving them clear direction and feedback, checking with suggestions and support, and continuing to motivate them to become star performers. You would like to spend more time with them, and possibly help them move into your high performer group, but there just isn't enough time.

- *Poor performer.* This group could represent about 10 percent of your employee population. If left unchecked, however, this can easily consume about 80 percent of a manager's time. These employees need to be managed a lot, which usually means performance coaching with specific improvement plans, time frames, and consequences clearly outlined.

If you don't deal with poor performers and others notice it, it may suck some of your average performers into what I call the "evil vortex of hell," and you might eventually find more than 10 percent of your employees in the poor performer category. When you don't deal with the poor performers, average performers often wonder why they should work so hard when they could simply get other people to help when they screw up and still get paid the same money. This problem perpetuates itself in a downward spiral until the group becomes unmanageable and an upper manager decides the only solution is to change the manager (i.e., you).

My advice to you is to deal with employees appropriately. This may mean having the honest conversation with them, performance coaching them, or guiding them towards their true calling, which could very well be with another organization. Over the years, I have identified many reasons why people don't address these issues, and the excuse I hear most often is that the bad behaviour will go away if you just ignore it. It usually does go away after several years when the employee finally retires or quits, but extensive damage will have already been done by then.

Leading Change

Imagine yourself taking on a new role. Do you come prepared with new ideas and opportunities for change and improvement? If so, you're probably ready for the change because you've thought about it, possibly had a key role in its design, and maybe even led such a change in the past. In a sense, you're at the forefront of the change curve. But what about the people you now lead? How do you get your staff to buy into your new vision (without grumbles of "It looks like someone read a new management book this weekend")?

One way to start is by understanding why your staff would reject your ideas. If you're new to the department, your fresh perspective may make certain changes obvious to you. These changes, and the areas of improvement they address, may not be so obvious to your team. If your team has done something for a long time, it's probably automatic or comfortable to them. This can easily make them reluctant to learn a new way, usually because of the effort it will take. Also, if they have regularly experienced what they define as success, they may fear change because they fear failure.

Successful change gurus, including Daryl R. Conner, author of *Managing at the Speed of Change*; William

Bridges, author of *The Way of Transition*; and John P. Kotter, author of *Leading Change*, have articulated various theories on leading change. Each of these authors provides guidelines for approaching and navigating your way through the change process, and all are worth reading. If you're about to embark on a change initiative that will have a direct or indirect impact on your staff, there are certain things you should keep in mind if you want to increase your chances of success. The steps that the experts propose are more extensive than what I have presented here, but for simplicity's sake, I recommend the following to get started:

1. Create a sense of urgency and clarity at the start. Be clear about why you need to make the change and what that change is. This is very important, as people are often reluctant to change when they don't know the reason for it. Even then, they can be resistant. Their understanding the importance of the change is critical to getting their support. Regardless, there will still be a lot of work to do because there are often many unknowns.

   In his book *Managing at the Speed of Change*, Daryl R. Conner discusses creating a "burning platform." I won't try to cover it here because I don't want to oversimplify a complicated concept, but I will say that it's worth having a look at the book for this concept alone. It demonstrates using urgency in the most extreme situations. The point I want to make is that you need to engage as many people as possible as willing participants in any change. If people can see the change is important to both the organization and themselves, you will have a greater chance of winning their support.

2. Include people as early as possible and make them part of the solution. Doing this creates a sense of ownership. The sooner people understand why a change is happening and how it will affect them, the greater the chance you will garner some support. As a manager, you will probably always have more information than your employees and will probably hear about any changes first.

   Your employees will likely be very concerned about how a change and the unknown factors of the change will affect them. It's always better if they hear information from you as early as possible so they don't hear things through the rumour mill of inaccurate information. Sometimes you can't provide as much information as you would like because of the wider implications of larger changes such as mergers or takeovers, but try to provide as much information as you can as soon as you can. Hopefully, the organization you work for will also understand the implications of not informing people as soon as possible.

The other aspect I've mentioned throughout this book is that the people who work closest to the clients or the company's production often have ideas about how to make things better. This means that good ideas for managing the change could come from your employees if you engage them early enough.

3. Ensure constant feedback on the progress of the change to reduce stress and fear. For the most part, stress and fear about unknowns are part of the change process, but you can lessen the impact by keeping people informed. As I mentioned above, there are times when certain information can't be shared—for example, when the change involves a takeover that may affect stock prices if information is leaked too soon or in the case of a merger that could involve layoffs. But in many cases, communicating to employees that a change is coming—the implementation of a new inventory tracking system, for example—will allow them to prepare for the change and provide assistance and insights into the implementation.

Change is better tolerated when it's collaborative. Change can be difficult for people, but it can help you build your team if you have clear communication, respectful relationships, adequate recognition, established trust, and ongoing engagement.

Over the past forty-two years, I have led or been involved in several change initiatives. Most of these changes were successfully completed, but many of them could have been more successful had the above-mentioned steps been better followed. One example of this is when I tried to change a shipping process early in my career.

One day it occurred to me that we could improve our shipping by using each of the shipping doors of our refrigerated cooler for multiple purposes instead of having specific doors assigned to specific delivery people. When a space at a shipping door became empty, we could immediately build a load and put it by that door. We could hang the appropriate route number on the outside of the door so the delivery person would know what door to use to pick up the products for the following day's delivery. It was a perfect plan. I could see it in my imagination with great clarity. The truck drivers would see the numbers as they arrived, back in at the appropriate door, load their vehicles, and then clear the way for the next truck. I thought it was brilliant!

I had special placards made up with all the route numbers and had hangers installed on the doors. I informed the entire shipping staff of the new steps. They all agreed and went about the new procedure the following day. My plan wasn't a complete failure, but I had overlooked some small but critical aspects that would have made the process a lot more successful. For example, some people were upset because the current loading process had been in place for almost fifteen years. They were comfortable with the longstanding process and didn't necessarily think we needed to change it. I also overlooked some obvious steps in the process, such as informing the drivers of the change and doing some research on the arrival of the trucks back at our depot. Some trucks arrived back at different times on different days, which meant that we needed to change the timing on those days. There were other issues as well that required some modification over the following few weeks, which caused grumbling and complaints.

Ultimately, my shipping process change proved to be a good decision, but it could have gone over a lot better. Here are some minor considerations I would include if I could do it over again:

1. I should have met and consulted with my crew earlier to get their input on the change. Although my staff ultimately agreed that the change was a good idea, it would have been a much smoother transition if I had received their feedback sooner rather than later.

2. I should have met with the delivery personnel to notify them of the change and get their unique perspective.

3. I should have set up a mechanism for ongoing

feedback so I could make improvements to the process and validate the importance of my staff's opinions.

As this example illustrates, even fairly minor change initiatives (i.e., not bigger adjustments such as those made to work schedules, pay structures, responsibilities, or accountability) can have wider effects. Changes can upset the normal flow that people have become accustomed to, which can cause stress, anxiety, and confusion. Imagine if you were trying to institute a major change such as a merger, which usually involves deep and far-reaching adjustments such as altered and/or increased workloads, unsettling layoffs, disruptive rescheduling, and/or new or expanded contracting. As a manager, how you lead change will influence your employees and your department. Draw upon the strategies and information in this book to help you strengthen your team, even in times of change, and improve your odds of success.

Chapter 8

Preparing for Rough Water Decision-Making or Walking the Plank

On any voyage you take, you run the risk of encountering rough water. With any job, project, or assignment you take on, you have to prepare yourself for when things don't go as planned. This doesn't mean you should spend your time imagining you'll hit an iceberg or be capsized by a tidal wave. Rather, you should simply plan adequately and anticipate potential problems. Being a manager means looking beyond what's happening on a given day. It means looking ahead, sometimes days, weeks, months, or years in advance.

You might think you'll make proper decisions to counteract certain situations that come up, but you don't need to leave every challenge to chance. If things go wrong and someone needs to make an important decision, your employees will look to you. You don't want to find yourself in a situation where your options become fewer until the only one left is to walk the plank.

Decision-Making

In a survey I conducted recently with a group of human resources professionals and senior managers from private and public firms, one of the questions asked them to identify the top five technical skills that are critical to a new manager. I was surprised to find the number one answer was decision-making, which topped other answers such as planning, priority-setting, performance management, driving results, labour and employee relations, budgeting, and recruitment, among other areas of management. The ability to make decisions and facilitate decision-making has become critical to organizations. I suspect this is in part due to the speed and ever-evolving nature of change happening everywhere.

When problems occur and it's something you haven't planned for, you need to make decisions, often decisively and sometimes with very little consultation. A manager's inability or unwillingness to make decisions is another key area that I've had subordinates and superiors regularly complain about. As we've discussed, it's best to consult with those closest to the situation whenever possible to seek their input, as they often have specific knowledge and/or a degree of expertise that might prove valuable when problems arise.

However, there may be times when such people aren't available. Managers still need to make decisions. Maybe it's in the middle of the night and you receive a call about an order that needs to be shipped but some of the product isn't available, or you receive a call from an important customer who is threatening to quit. You gather the information available, weigh the risks, look at options, and then make the best decision you can. Sometimes you will need to defer a decision until you gather more information, or sometimes you come up with a decision that corrects a situation in two or more parts. For example, in the case of the product availability, you might decide to ship the product you have on hand and then send the remainder of the order by a special delivery as soon as it arrives. There is usually something you can do. Part of that is to communicate your decision to the people who are most affected by the decision. Why? To let employees know what has taken place. Plus, you can often use these situations as learning experiences for others.

Talking to subordinates about the course of action you took when you had to make a decision helps teach them how they might make a decision when they find themselves in a similar situation when you aren't around. Sometimes the decisions you make won't go as well as you hoped. It happens to all of us. Assuming it's not a decision that will drive the company into bankruptcy, you will use it as a learning experience, and it will reinforce the importance of including others as often as possible.

What Can You Control?

Let's look at what I simply call "doing what you can do." New managers often run into a dilemma where they get frustrated by what they can and cannot do. It sometimes happens when they attend one of my programs. They get all excited about new concepts or new leadership principles they've learned, but then their heads drop and they slump in their chairs. "I would do it," they say, "but my boss wouldn't support it…." Or they mention they don't have the money in the budget or mention the union won't allow it or mention some other expected barrier. That's when they get my standard response: "What can you do?"

One of the key lessons I have learned over the years is that you rarely get 100 percent support in any decision. So you look for doorways or access points and simply focus on the things you can do. In his book *Stepping Up*, John Izzo writes that if you wait for the perfect plan, you might wait forever, so do something, do anything, even if you can't directly influence the thinking of those around you.

I recently facilitated a leadership program. It was six days in total and ran in two-day slots spaced three weeks apart. Mary, one of the participants, was from outside the organization that hosted the program. On the fourth day, she asked if she could chat with me after class. When we met, she seemed down, or at least different from the first three days when she seemed inspired and excited about participating. She explained to me that her boss had been a real supporter of her participating in the program and had encouraged her to go. However, when she sat down with him after the second day to bring him up to speed on what she'd learned so far, he said it was just a bunch of crap and that the real way to manage people is to kick ass, take names, and don't take any prisoners.

This shocked Mary, as her boss was fully aware of the program and had reviewed the course curriculum with her before she signed up for it. The program covered concepts on influence, collaboration, coaching, and other current leadership thinking. Mary felt blindsided and wondered if she should continue taking the program, as it was now apparent her boss didn't support these concepts.

I recommended that she should ask herself, "What can I do?" I then explained to her that this would probably not be the last time she would face a challenge like this. If she didn't agree with her boss, she had several options. She could

1. confront her boss (possibly limiting her career),
2. ignore the situation (possibly creating frustration),
3. follow his advice (possibly stunting growth opportunities),
4. look for another job (if the situation really challenged her values), or
5. ask the question, "What can I do?"

Mary said that she would take a few days to think about my suggestion. When she returned a few weeks later for day five, she asked to talk to me at the conclusion of the day. When I met with her again, she told me she had gone home after our first discussion and thought about it. Actually, she admitted to contemplating it in some detail for several days. She had ultimately decided to take my advice, and she tried it out with her own direct reports and peers.

Mary set up one-on-one meetings with her employees to outline her long-term vision for her operating group. She asked for their support and what she needed to provide them to be successful. She set up ongoing monthly 30-minute one-on-one meetings so she could update people on the company's progress and to get updates from each of them. She admitted that the discussions weren't all smooth sailing, as some of the employees were very skeptical about her motives, but people for the most part seemed willing to give it a try.

Mary also learned some things from her own leadership perspective. She realized that people could still have an impact even under very trying situations if they focused on what they could do. She also learned that she didn't want to manage the same way her boss managed, which was reminiscent of the old autocratic style of management that was more prevalent before the eighties. Mary said that this would also affect her long-term goals, including whether she would stay with the company or search for an organization with a management philosophy akin to her own.

In any situation where you face a challenge beyond your control (e.g., there's really nothing you can do about it because it was a decision that upper management made), ask yourself, "What can I do?" The answer may simply be, "Very little," but you could at least adjust your attitude or approach. The idea here is that you can always do something.

Looking Beyond Yourself

As I've mentioned several times already, you are no longer an individual contributor when you become a manager. Even if you maintain some line duties, you now also manage people who are meant to be your resources for completing certain work. What you're ultimately trying to do is build a team that can contribute to the organization more successfully than a group of people who just happen to work in the same department. This will require your assessments in determining how people fit into the landscape of your department and how they fit into what you're trying to accomplish. This may include providing additional role clarity or job training.

Thankfully, it's unlikely you'll have to build a new team from scratch. You're likely to inherit a team that has worked in the same department for a long time. Your team has probably seen a few managers come and go and has no doubt formulated their collective opinion about the kind of manager they prefer. If their previous managers were strong, fair, and honest, you will likely encounter a team with high expectations. If their pervious managers were dishonest, selfish, single-minded, and/or unfair in their treatment of employees, your team will likely welcome a new management style…or perhaps they will be completely untrusting of anyone new because they assume all managers act the same way. If their previous manager had taken a laissez-faire approach, it will probably be difficult for you to bring changes to improve productivity, quality, and customer service in the early stages.

In early 2007, I worked with a company in New York, and my experience with a particular manager highlights these points. After completing undergraduate and graduate degrees in chemistry at a prestigious US university, Gurmeet joined a pharmaceutical company. While attending school, she had also worked part-time in her father's retail business. Her company had hired me to provide managerial training and development, which included coaching individual managers. I was very impressed with her technical knowledge and her knowledge in dealing with the emotional and motivational aspects of employees. She understood empathy, asking questions to develop understanding, using mistakes as a way to learn, and making tough decisions when necessary. Her involvement in the class demonstrated that she believed in and used all of these techniques. She wasn't just regurgitating them from a book to impress her classmates or me.

On a break, Gurmeet asked to meet with me for a coaching session as soon as I could find time for her. In our session, she shared the following story. She had been hired as a junior chemist three years earlier, which was fairly standard hiring practice for the organization. She was part of a team of fourteen other chemists of varying experience and tenure with the organization. The manager who hired her was extremely nice and they got along very well. Gurmeet received work assignments that were, in many cases, more advanced than she had been used to, and she worked upwards of sixty hours each week to complete many of the tasks. Despite this, she told me that she loved the opportunity to learn so much in such a short period. She said that she didn't get a lot of direction from her manager. Usually, the most instruction she got was, "Go ahead and try it; you will be fine."

Many of Gurmeet's colleagues didn't work as long as she did or were often away at conferences, presenting some of their research findings. When her boss announced that he was leaving the organization for personal reasons, the general manager approached Gurmeet and asked if she would like to take over as the supervisor. She jumped at the chance because this had been a long-term goal of hers.

The general manager then provided her with the following background information: Her manager hadn't actually left for personal reasons but was rather asked to leave for what they believed was his "lack of management with his team." He was a nice guy, but he was absent much of the time and didn't hold people accountable for the work the organization required. Consequently, his department had the highest expenses but the least productivity in producing new product lines.

As Gurmeet reflected on the general manager's comments, she realized that she had been very busy because everyone else had been working on their own personal projects much of the time. Although everyone was happy, they weren't really contributing to the company's bottom line. She wasn't part of a team working towards a common goal but rather a group of individuals who showed up at the same workplace each day. They did the minimum required work to get by while the junior team members who hadn't yet figured out the routine did most of the required work.

By the time Gurmeet approached me for a coaching session, she had been managing her team for three months. She told me that the situation with her team wasn't improving. In fact, things had been getting even worse because productivity was still low and now people were angry and disagreeable. Gurmeet simply said to me, "At least before, even when productivity was low, people seemed to get along together. Now, no one even talks."

As a new manager, Gurmeet was trying to deal with a team that had been given a great deal of freedom for quite a while. The previous manager had acted more like a social club director than a business leader. She was finding it very difficult to implement changes to improve productivity and relationships. Her progress had been slow, and she was looking for additional strategies. This wasn't a typical 9-to-5 workforce; these were highly trained specialists in their field who had been given a fair amount of autonomy from both a work perspective and a personal perspective.

Gurmeet and I talked about taking a multifaceted approach because there were several patterns of behaviour that needed changing. We spent some time identifying the key areas of concern, and she ended up taking the following approach.

First, she re-established the company's purpose and what each employee's role was in contributing to it. She focused on role clarity, as she understood the importance of having each employee clearly understand his or her specific role. She also outlined the implications of people not doing their jobs and the impact it would have on the organization and their individual careers.

On top of that, Gurmeet explained to her team what she needed to do, what her expectations were, and how she intended to lead people through this change. She was sure to let people know that there would still be time allotted to some personal research and to attend conferences, but she would need to approve this, as their jobs as chemists must be completed first.

In addition, Gurmeet also scheduled regular one-on-one meetings to track progress, continue open conversations, and express her confidence in the team's ability to meet her expectations. She decided to avoid group meetings so the team wouldn't gang up on her.

Gurmeet also met with her manager before starting the meetings to make sure she had his full support, as she assumed that people might start going above her head to her boss, looking for a sympathetic ear regarding any changes they didn't like. He was in full support of her approach and also let her know that he wouldn't be concerned if some people left the company as a result of the changes she wanted to institute. He said there were many capable candidates in the open market who might prove a better fit into the culture they were trying to build.

I worked with Gurmeet over several months. It was a tough slog for her, especially early on. People threatened to quit, threatened to go to her boss, threatened to go to the president (we already had that covered), and in some cases tried to sabotage their work, saying they had too much to do and couldn't possibly meet the unrealistic time lines.

The fact was that Gurmeet was simply asking people to do the jobs they had been hired to do. She was holding them accountable for their jobs instead of simply letting them work mostly on their personal projects. She had estimated that people's actual division of work in the past was typically ten to fifteen hours a week on their assigned work duties and twenty-five to thirty hours a week on personal projects. She was driving towards flipping those numbers.

Over the months, Gurmeet experienced a lot of pushback and complaints, but she didn't relent. Three of the chemists left. One was fairly senior, and they were sorry to see him go, but people saw that Gurmeet was steadfast in her commitment after he was gone. They also saw that she had the support of upper management. The tide started to shift, and productivity grew steadily, and here's the funny thing: so did people's personal research efforts. In other words, people became much more productive *overall*, not just towards the company's goals. As things settled down, Gurmeet also found that she could grant people more time to work on personal projects if they were ahead on their work-related projects.

In the end, Gurmeet made some unpopular decisions, but they were critical to the company and had the support of upper management. She stuck by those decisions until a point when she could recognize good work and reward extra personal research time. She continued to let people know what her expectations were and regularly checked in with them to make sure they were on target, but she also made sure they had the resources to support their efforts.

After six months, Gurmeet started up group meetings again so they could discuss department issues and also recognize people for their accomplishments. It was a lot of work for Gurmeet, and she was unable to reduce the time she spent at work for almost a year, but sometimes that's what it takes.

Chapter 9

From Sea Legs to Sea Dogs: Building and Developing Your Team

If you're part of a ship's deck crew and want to advance through the ranks (and you have the skill, experience, and desire), you could progress from ordinary seaman to able seaman to boatswain. Future promotions beyond that might include third mate, second mate, and maybe even first mate. There are many different crews or departments on any ship, including engineering and stewards. The size and complexity of these crews depend on the size and complexity of the ship.

The real difference between working on a ship versus an organization on land is that instead of firing you if things don't work out, they simply throw you overboard. Just kidding. There are, however, many similarities in that people in both instances need to show a desire and aptitude towards advancing. They have to develop certain skills, gain experience, and in most cases demonstrate some ability to work with people, especially if they're taking on a management position.

Most people who join organizations don't expect to retire from the same job they started with. Some have definite career goals they want to achieve, while some are more laissez-faire in their approach. Others aren't interested at all in promotions or more responsibility; they just want to do their jobs.

There are probably times when great teams just happen, where the right people come together with all the right skills and drive to make a world-class team. I don't know about you, but I've never been part of a great team that just came together. Sure, I've worked with great teams, but it was always due to the manager's hard work, which included such things as hiring competent people, setting clear expectations, holding people accountable for their actions and their work, creating an engaging and empowering work environment, and sometimes replacing employees who didn't fit into the team.

A critical factor of successful teams that often gets overlooked in unsuccessful teams is each team member's need for ongoing learning and development. In my coaching and consulting sessions with managers, I've heard the many reasons for not developing their people, including "It's not my job," "I don't have time," "The company doesn't have money to send people on courses," and "If we train them, they'll leave for a better job." Believe me, if you decide not to train and develop people, the likelihood of losing your best and brightest will happen sooner than if you did train and develop them. This is especially true when it comes to information technology and systems staff. They tend to expect constant access to training and upgrading.

Developing Others

Through all of my years in business, I've often been asked, "Whose responsibility is it to develop employees?" There's no simple answer to that question. Can someone really make a difference in the development and success of others?

Think of how this works in sports. In any amateur sports league, the equipment is relatively the same for each team, and the number of players is usually the same. The players usually have varying degrees of skill, but their membership on one team over another is generally random. To some degree, the success of a team depends on how the players are managed and coached. A coach's ability to bring out the best in players can directly influence their chances of winning a championship. Coaches are important, as evidenced by their high turnover rate on professional teams that experience multiple losing seasons.

In her book *Multipliers: How the Best Leaders Make Everyone Smarter*, Liz Wiseman examines the effect leaders can have as either "multipliers" who help build the capability of their teams or "diminishers" who drain capability from their teams. Multipliers build people up. They assume that people are smart and will stay smart. They have high expectations and will challenge people. They invest in people and are a talent magnet. Diminishers, on the other hand, can be empire builders and know-it-alls. They can also be micromanagers who involve people in decisions only after the decisions have been made.

This doesn't mean that multipliers are soft and diminishers are tough. Most multipliers are tough, but their toughness is directed more at assisting you in being the best you can be. Fortunately, I haven't worked for too many diminishers, at least not for long. This next story relates one of my experiences about a diminisher I had the misfortune of working for many years ago.

I remember a conversation I had with the president of the division I worked in when I first started in business. I could never figure out how he got his job. I think he was promised a senior position when an international conglomerate acquired his father's business. The one thing I was certain of was his lack of leadership skills, specifically development skills. At one point, he told me, "You complete your education in high school or university and then you go to work, which is where you really learn the things you need. The education part is just something you need to do before you get on with things." He then gave me one of his old books from university to read. He told me that was where I could find the technical information I needed to know about the business. That's it. Not exactly a stellar employee development program.

This president's lack of interest in developing people has stuck with me throughout my career. He didn't believe he was at all accountable for developing his employees. I thought the best thing for the organization was for him to get out of the business as soon as possible—thankfully, he did.

Think about it this way. If you work for someone who diminishes you, will you ever be at your best? Will you want to work as hard as you can and treat the organization like you have ownership in it? I doubt it.

This topic has been debated for some time. Whose responsibility is it to develop staff? Is it the employee's sole responsibility? Is it the responsibility of the organization? Is it a shared responsibility?

I believe that education is a lifelong process that extends beyond formal schooling. I believe it's a shared responsibility with each party making a full commitment to the process. This process benefits the organization, as its employees increase their skills and capabilities. It also benefits the employees in many ways. For example, it increases their opportunities for advancement and improves their value to the organization. This can lead to higher income, increased job security, and greater job satisfaction. When an organization invests in its employees, it makes many people feel like they matter.

Some organizations take a very cautious approach to formal training (e.g., paying for expensive seminars, conferences, MBA programs, etc.) because they cynically believe employees will leave the company once they acquire advanced training and/or education. Although educated employees certainly do leave after a period of development, it's not the norm. Conversely, when an organization invests in formal development, it can pay in dividends by retaining their best and brightest.

It's important to understand that formal training is

only one form of development. Many development opportunities lie within the hands of direct supervisors. These include coaching, mentoring, job sharing, and job shadowing. Although managers often overlook these development methods, they can be among the most important and least expensive.

Consider these questions to get you thinking about employee development:

- Are you actively involved in the development plans of your employees?

- Do you know whether your employees are interested in developing in different areas?

- Are you currently involved in coaching or mentoring any of your employees or employees from other departments?

- Have you encouraged employees to look for mentors outside of their departments?

In short, development options can include formal development programs, such as external programs or courses delivered by universities, colleges, and professional training organizations, or informal and inexpensive methods of coaching and mentoring.

Mentoring isn't anything new, but in some organizations it has become a more planned aspect or regular part of operations. In two organizations I worked for, we ran a mentoring program once a year. It was a voluntary program where employees would identify someone they wanted to mentor under. If the mentor agreed to it, a series of meetings were set up over a six-month period where the mentor and mentee shared experiences. The organizational development department provided resources such as meeting planners, agendas, and topic sheets for people to use. There was also a mentor/mentee orientation session and kick-off, and the program ended with a final celebration meeting. This kind of program isn't necessarily to prepare someone for a specific job, but it gives new or junior employees a look at the organization from a different perspective.

Over the years, I've found that mentors gain as much learning and insight from the sessions as mentees do. Mentoring doesn't need to be formal or extensively planned. As a manager, you could simply identify people in your organization who have a lot to teach your newer high-potential employees and then find ways for them to interact regularly.

Coaching, on the other hand, has become a buzzword in business. Organizations sometimes hire external executive coaches for their senior employees, especially newly promoted ones. However, what we're seeing more of is coaching used in job descriptions for managers. It's not always defined, so always ask what coaching means in the company you work for and be prepared to offer your own definition. For me, in very simple terms, a leadership coach assists employees with finding their own answers through a series of questions and insights based on experience, knowledge, and expertise.

Coaching is much more complex than mentoring. I will explore it in more detail in my next book. Let's just say that managers don't have to have all the answers all the time, but they need to help people find their own solutions for their own journey. Some organizations have even gone to the extent of hiring internal coaches and training their own people to act as coaches to support managers. I still believe that the best solution is the idea of having the manager as coach.

Delegation

One of the greatest roadblocks to the successful transition from doer to leader is an inability to delegate or a fear of delegating authority to those who report to you.

Delegation means not only assigning work to people under your charge but also providing the tools, support, and authority necessary to complete the task or a portion of it. An unwillingness to delegate is sometimes rooted in the fear of losing control, and sometimes it's a lack of trust in the ability of others to successfully complete tasks. Regardless of the reason, there is very little chance for long-term success if a manager is unable to delegate.

Remember, employees are your most valuable resource. It will be difficult to complete all the work you're responsible for if you don't engage them. It's about setting reasonable parameters in the early stages and expanding the responsibility as employees gain your trust.

You also need to consider the worst that can happen if things don't go exactly the way you planned. I'm reminded of a personal story that illustrates my point.

At a family barbecue we were hosting, I asked my new son-in-law to handle the grilling duties—a "passing of the tongs," so to speak—and he accepted. I was pleased because this would give me time to socialize. I started the barbecue, provided him with all the tools, and had all the meal ingredients at the ready. I then proceeded to stand over him and tell him how to flip over each piece of meat, how long to cook it for, and how to place it on the platter when it was ready.

After the barbecue, as he and my daughter were getting ready to leave, I thanked him for his assistance. He responded with a smile and told me that he had never been micromanaged at a barbecue before. I suddenly realized that I had set him up to be successful at the job but hadn't provided him with the accountability and trust to get it done on his own. I knew he would have done a good job because I had seen him do it before at another barbecue. Why was I so reluctant to relinquish the job to him? It's amazing how simple illustrative stories like these play out time and time again in personal and professional life.

Consider the following questions to help you determine your ability (and willingness) to delegate:

1. On a scale of 1 to 10, with 1 being poor and 10 being outstanding, how would you rate your delegation skills?

2. When you delegate, do you provide people with the following?

   a. Tools and resources (e.g., hammers, screw-drivers, computers, training and development, information, other team members, etc.)

   b. Support (e.g., expectations, trust, ongoing feedback, reassurance, freedom from a fear of failure, etc.)

   c. Authority (e.g., giving credit for success, offering learning discussions after failures, etc.)

If your delegation skills are lacking and you find yourself doing your employees' work for them, what can you do? How do you move from performing like an individual contributor to performing like a delegating, goal-oriented leader?

One thing I recommend to new managers is to spend some time in the early stages watching people and asking questions. In Chapter 5, we discussed management by wandering around (MBWA). Many managers spend too much of their time sitting in their offices, reading reports or doing other paperwork. What they need to do is get out among the staff, whether it's on the factory floor or in a sales office, or get out and talk to the customers. This is where you find out what's really going on. And guess what? You get to do it for free, and you can often discover things first by talking directly to the people doing the work or the people buying your products or services.

I worked for a manager in my early career who regularly went on walks through the plant and shipping areas, sometimes if he arrived early in the morning or if he stayed late at night. He didn't do it to check up on people. He tried to keep his finger on the pulse of the business. He would interact with everyone and find out what was going on. It also made the employees who worked in the plant happy because they knew they had a chance to interact with the top guy.

Believe me, I have worked with and for organizations where the employees have never met or even seen the top person in the company. As a new manager, whether you've been promoted from within the department or have come from outside the organization, you need to view your department from a different perspective. You need to view it from the perspective of a manager and leader. It's time for you to look beyond how you would do something and extend it to how "we" can make it better. You've been given a valuable resource: people. Your job is to maximize their productivity without compromising quality or doing anybody any harm.

Positive Recognition

It seems that every employee survey I've organized over the past thirty years has listed recognition (or the lack thereof) as one of the top five areas for improvement. Yet, when I talk to managers, they all tell me they recognize people for the work they do. When I ask them for examples of how they recognize the performance of their employees, they often fumble for a minute before admitting they could probably do a better job of it.

Why do so many people struggle with recognition?

Reason	My Response
"I don't have time to recognize people for good work."	Good managers always find time to thank their employees. If you can't find the time to recognize your employees, you might be in the wrong job. Assess your strengths and goals. Be sure to acknowledge your employees for their commitment and the quality of their work.
"It's their job. I shouldn't have to thank them for doing a job they're paid to do."	Consistently acknowledging good work is a reinforcement technique that demonstrates to employees that they matter.
"I don't have the authority to give them extra money, and that's the only real reward."	Money is a powerful motivator, but most organizations don't have unlimited monetary incentives. Fortunately, research supports the idea that money isn't the only real reward. Small tokens of thanks are also appreciated and can be used as a motivational tool if used genuinely and on a timely basis.
"I don't want to look soft."	Ruling by force is no longer considered good managerial practice. People respect and feel more connected to those who give them genuine compliments on a job well done.

If you recognize the positive efforts and achievements of your employees, they will be more likely to respect you as a manager. Genuine gratitude rather than shallow acknowledgement will reinforce positive relationships and motivate your staff. Recognition also needs to be timely. Try to recognize good performance as soon as possible. Also, make sure you know your people well enough so you can tailor your recognition to each individual. For instance, some people like to be recognized in public or in front of their peers, while others prefer to receive private acknowledgement.

To improve your positive recognition efforts, consider the following questions.

1. Do you look for people doing things well so you can acknowledge them?

2. Do you know the best way to recognize your employees?

3. Who have you recognized recently? Who should you have recognized but didn't?

4. Have you aligned your recognition with the clear expectations you set for the organizational goals?

When I talk to managers about recognizing their employees, they sometimes immediately jump to saying, "I don't have the money." There are many different ways to recognize employees other than giving them a monetary reward. It's nice when you can provide this, but bonuses for performance are often simply a part of compensation structures for organizations that can afford them.

What we're talking about here is recognition that happens as soon as possible after an outcome. For example, just before leaving to go home at the end of the day, an employee finds a mistake in a report that's being presented tomorrow. Instead of saying, "Well, that's not my job," she stays late and fixes the report. As soon as you find out about it, you thank her for her extra effort and tell her you appreciate that she volunteered to stay late to help the company avoid an inconvenient, costly, and/or embarrassing mistake. You might also explain what the specific consequences would have been had the report been submitted with such an error. By doing this, you demonstrate your appreciation for going above and beyond expectations. In the future, she will probably be more likely to repeat such behaviour if a similar situation happens.

There are all kinds of ways to say thank you with little or no expense. These include everything from a face-to-face thank you, thank-you cards, phone calls, or email messages. You could give employees a gift card to their favourite coffee shop or, even better, take them for a coffee. This will give you an opportunity to get to know them a bit better and for them to get to know you. The idea here is that you don't let these great opportunities slip away. Recognize people for going beyond what you expect of them and thank them for the good work they do every day.

Making People Feel Like They Matter

If my coaching practice has taught me anything, it's that most people want to feel like they matter. They want their boss (and more broadly their organization) to value their presence and their contributions. I've had many discussions with people who say that the only things that matter are money and power. This may be true in many cases, but I have a hard time believing it based on what I've heard from many people over the years. This is especially the case when compensation meets primary needs because most people would say they would like to earn more. However, I've noticed that once people receive a level of compensation that provides them a decent amount of comfort, they become more invested in their jobs and want to contribute to the organization to make it better. Moreover, they want their boss and even their boss' boss to recognize their contributions.

A few years ago, I conducted an exit interview with Josie, who had shocked her manager with her resignation. Her manager really wanted to understand why she was leaving because he had believed that she was happy in her position. She was a high performer, and he felt she had the potential to move to a senior position. She had told him that she was very happy with the organization but that her new position offered her more opportunity for advancement. Josie's manager believed there was an underlying reason for her departure, and he wanted to understand it. I contacted her and explained that we asked people to attend exit interviews to help us understand employee perspectives of our organization, including areas that need improvement.

Upon meeting with her, I congratulated Josie on her new job and asked her if she was excited about the new opportunity. What she told me was quite interesting. She said that she didn't want to leave the organization and was actually taking a bit of a pay cut in doing so. For the most part, she had been very happy with her opportunities, her pay, and her co-workers. She then admitted that she couldn't move forward in the organization because she didn't feel that she mattered there. She went on to explain that knowing that her work and her contributions to the organization made a difference and were valued would make her feel like she mattered.

This made me think back over my previous forty-two years in business and the many times I've had conversations with people. I couldn't remember ever hearing anyone say, "I need to matter." I guess maybe I've heard people say it in different ways, but I've never heard it said that way. It was somewhat different from what I'd traditionally thought about recognition. I was used to thinking about it in more tangible terms such as acknowledging that you finished a report ahead of schedule or that you stayed late to get the job done or that you otherwise went above and beyond the call of duty. This is stuff you can see. It's measurable. What Josie was talking about seemed very different, but it resonated with me, and I could understand it. Maybe it's based on the different values of the next generation. Maybe it's that they're more willing to talk about this stuff. I don't know for sure, but it's something I think needs further investigation, and it's something you need to be aware of as a manager. It's definitely big picture stuff.

Below are some questions that might help guide you in conversations with employees when the opportunity presents itself. You don't need to ask all of these questions, and you may even have some of your own. The idea is to engage people in conversations. Share a bit about yourself, and they will probably share a bit about themselves. In a sense, it's like giving up a bit of yourself. Some of this goes to the heart of trying to establish a relationship. Sure, we have different jobs to do, and sometimes you have to make unpopular decisions as a manager, but we are all people working towards certain goals, whether it's advancing our careers, raising a family, saving for a first home, giving back to the community, or preparing for retirement.

Asking questions is a way to make people understand that you're interested in them and that they matter. People aren't just a number, a faceless person in the crowd of people checking their brains at the door when they arrive and then picking them up on the way out when they head home. The world has changed, and managers today need to consider how they will change and adapt to the new workforce. The next wave of workers hitting the workforce and who will eventually take over for the previous generations of baby boomers and Gen Xers are the millennials, and they are about ten million strong in Canada, about 27.5 percent of the population. As of 2015, they made up about 35 percent of Canada's civilian workforce, and this should exceed 50 percent by 2020.[2] Maybe you're one of them. How do you want to be managed and how does that fit into how organizations operate today? You need to learn how your employees want to be managed and led!

The following questions will help inform some of your decisions on how to proceed.

1. What do you really know about your employees (hobbies, outside interests, etc.)?

2. Have you ever considered asking the question "What are you passionate about?"

3. How often do you ask employees for their help on something outside of their normal responsibilities?

4. What kind of information do your employees need to hear from you?

5. What do you need to hear from your boss? Have you told your boss that this is the kind of feedback you need?

---

[2] Scott, Graham F. 2015. ªMillennial Workers Now Outnumber Gen Xers and Boomers.º *Canadian Business*. June 4, 2015. https://www.canadianbusiness.com/innovation/the-millennial-majority-workforce/.

Instilling a culture of learning and leadership in which employees are respected, educated, developed, recognized, and engaged will help them feel like they matter. This kind of culture reinforces the worth of employees, and it also improves productivity and job satisfaction. As a manager, you will likely have at least one of these aspects as a personal, professional, or organizational goal. By working on these aspects, you will be better equipped to stay the managerial course and achieve success.

Section 4

Returning to Harbour: Your Captain's Log

Each ship eventually returns to harbour after a long voyage—at least the crew, the passengers, and the ship's owner hope it will. Upon the ship's return, the captain makes a final entry in the captain's log for the trip. This sums up the events of the trip, identifies anything learned, and helps preparations for the next voyage.

For a manager, returning to harbour can signify many things. It could mean a return to your office after a performance discussion between you, a union representative, and a disgruntled employee. It could mean returning to your office after a marathon meeting with colleagues about cost-cutting measures for the next budget. It could mean coming home to your family after a long day at work. Regardless of whether you're the captain of an ocean liner or a manager of a small group of employees, returning to harbour is an important time. It's when you get a chance to collect your thoughts, impressions, and lessons from the day. It's a time to contemplate what went well, what you accomplished, and what you would do differently next time. This time of self-reflection is an invaluable learning experience where you can evaluate what happened so you can repeat positive processes in the future while avoiding bad or ineffective ones. This type of reflection basically allows you to think about the areas you want to develop and work on so you can prepare for the next day, or your next voyage.

A few years ago, I was working with a senior executive for a large multinational corporation, and he mentioned to me that the first thing he did when he woke up in the morning was think about the day ahead of him. He would plan out his day in great detail in his mind, including any upcoming meetings he had. He'd think about what he might say and how he would answer questions he might encounter at the meetings. He told me that this eliminated a lot of the known concerns from his mind because he felt he had a plan. He knew there would be things that would happen that he couldn't plan for, but he felt he could better deal with them if he had the known parts of his day already planned out.

In a sense, we carry each meeting, each day, and each experience forward with us. As such, we should ask ourselves whether we learned anything from it and ask ourselves what we will do to do make it better.

Chapter 10

Captain's Log: What Did You Learn?

You've returned to harbour and made your final entry into the log about the trip. You've identified what happened, what went well, what didn't go so well, and what areas warrant further investigation.

Now you start to look at the changes and improvements you might want to make, and you start to understand what you're good at and what you're not good at. You think a lot about your strengths and weaknesses. You might even ask some people who know you well what they believe they are. Regardless, you start to think about the things you want to do differently, the things you want to keep doing, and maybe even the things you want to stop doing if they're not adding value to the organization and your career.

Another thing I have learned over the years is that successful leaders understand what they do well. They also often understand what they don't do well, but they tend not to care or spend much time worrying about those things. More often than not, they hire people to do those things instead. They mostly rely on what they're really good at.

In the early stages of your career, as you move and progress up the ladder of success, you will likely rely on the things you're good at. At the same time, you should understand your areas of weakness, as they could become fatal flaws if you leave them unchecked.

A fatal flaw is anything that could have a negative or career-limiting impact. For example, I once had the opportunity (or should I say the misfortune?) of working with an extremely smart person who had a great ability for coming up with ideas and solutions for every problem. Sometimes these were good ideas and sometimes they weren't. What she didn't realize was that she gave the impression that her opinion was the only one that mattered, that she needed to be viewed as the smartest person in the room while other ideas were discounted. This eventually led to her being despised by her colleagues and eventually being removed from her position. Fortunately, she was provided with an outplacement program when she left the company, and discussions with the outplacement consultant helped identify these issues. She took them to heart and mended her ways, and last I heard she was managing a high-performance team in a high-tech company and was doing very well. She was able to accept the feedback and make adjustments. More often than not people can't or won't change.

There's an old saying: When you overvalue your own contributions to the organization while discounting the contributions of others, you put the organization and yourself at great risk. It's not just what you do but how you do it. The difference between a new manager and an experienced manager is that a new manager can't necessary rely on current skills to get to the next level because complexity and politics often play more of a role the next level up.

What Got You Here Won't Keep You Here (or Necessarily Get You to the Next Place)

In your new role as a manager, you will likely carry out the directions of your own manager. It's unlikely that you will have the amount of decision-making autonomy you thought you would when you were promoted, but this is a good thing in the early stages. Consider yourself lucky if you receive a fair amount of guidance in the first six months to a year in your new position. Each rung you climb on the organizational ladder requires different skill sets to achieve success. At the first level of management, you can expect the following:

- Your immediate boss largely dictates your activities. You will often carry out jobs, objectives, or goals set for you.

- Your boss will usually determine your budgets, major projects, and long-term human resources strategies.

- Your goals and objectives will tend to be short-term, often with completion dates within weeks or months. Very seldom will your goals, or the goals of your operating group, extend beyond one year.

- Most of your work will be based on day-to-day activities with very little attention given to long-term strategic work.

I have met many frontline managers who have been in the same position for ten or twenty years because they were happy and felt successful in the role. If you want to move to the next level in an organization, you need to start preparing for that job when you begin your first role as a manager. Every time you talk to your boss or someone else more senior than you in the organization or with another organization, you're interviewing and being observed. As you move up in an organization, execution is still important, but *how* you get things done becomes more important—for example, how you forecast change in the competition and markets, how you allocate limited resources, how you take on increasing responsibility, how you find innovative and creative solutions to problems of increasing complexity and risk to the organization, and how you manage a greater span of control, to name a few.

For the most part, everything is just bigger as you rise among the ranks. This sometimes includes the egos of leaders. (I'll address this more in my next book.) Remember, this is about your career. You need to look after it because nobody else will, at least not to the extent you can. I think the world has changed enough over the past couple of decades that everyone now realizes people won't get everything perfect all the time. All of us are constantly learning, recalibrating, adjusting, and trying things from different perspectives. Regardless, none of us can rest on past achievements if we want to keep moving forward.

Often, the best way to find out about yourself beyond self-reflection is to ask and observe others who have been successful and are in more senior positions. The following questions will help guide you through this process.

1. Ask the person who promoted you why they made the decision. What skills did they recognize in you?

2. How do senior positions differ from yours? How do those in senior positions do their jobs? Keep this in mind as you work on long-term goals.

3. What skills, talents, and knowledge are valued by your organization? Observe what gets rewarded and work with a mentor to help you figure this out.

As you uncover the answers to these questions, you can start to formulate a development plan. This will likely lead to more questions such as the following:

1. What were the skills you demonstrated that got you promoted?

2. Did you regularly receive recognition for these skills or did you just learn about this recently?

3. Do you need to strengthen any of these skills?

4. Were any skills you thought you were good at not mentioned?

5. How does your skill set match with what senior leaders do? For example, if your planning ability was something identified as a strength, is it something that senior leaders are good at? Is it something valued by the organization?

These questions are important. Although most of us want to be original and have autonomy, when we work for any organization, a certain amount of conformity needs to take place. This doesn't mean we should ignore our ethics or value systems and comply with every request, but it does mean we will have to do certain things. For example, as a manager, you will need to do such things as schedule shifts, do annual performance reviews, make sure daily work gets completed, coach employees with substandard work behaviour, ensure health and safety standards are being met, etc. You may, however, have some flexibility on how you make decisions—for example, who to include in the decisions (and when to include them) and how to allocate resources, including moving people around depending on work demands.

As I mentioned earlier, managers shouldn't sit and wait for their bosses to let them know when they're ready for their next move or promotion. They must look ahead and anticipate. It's like hockey legend Wayne Gretzky's analogy: "Skate to where the puck is going, not where it has been." You need to look forward and gather as much information as possible about yourself and the organization so you can systematically plan out your career rather than take a haphazard approach.

Remember, this is your career. You need to own it and take full responsibility for your actions and development if you want to receive promotions. Another thing to keep in mind is that sometimes there won't be opportunities for advancement on your schedule, so you will have to make a decision to either stay and wait or seek opportunities elsewhere. Also consider that upgrading your skills and keeping ahead of the curve might be required just to keep the job you've got, never mind a promotion.

Chapter 11

Captain's Log: Developing Yourself

You've been sitting in the captain's cabin, completing the final entries in your log about your recent voyage. You've also started to make a list of the things you've learned along the way. You decided there are things you need to keep doing and things you need to start doing. There are even some things you need to stop doing all together because they're not adding any value. You're now looking at ways to start doing new things, and you want to strengthen some of the skills you're already using.

You realize that you're fairly knowledgeable as far as technical skills are concerned, partly because you've landed the managerial job and are currently doing it. But when it comes to leading people, maneuvering the organization, and finding some balance between your work life and personal life, you could use some help. So where do you go for help?

It's easy to forget yourself when you get into a position of managing others. You can get lost in the world of everyone else's issues and the constant pressure to meet organizational goals and objectives. Welcome to the real world. But, honestly, within the context of the decision you've made to take on a role in management, you need to find some balance. First, let me be frank: I don't believe that a true balance can exist between work life and personal life if you want to be a successful manager, so don't go into management if you want that kind of balance. What I mean is finding *some* balance where you can find the time to do the things that are necessary to sustain some normality in life. Balance will also ebb and flow depending on what stage of life you're in, whether it's the early stages of building your career, you're mid-career, you're a mid-level manager or a senior executive, etc.

Inspiring Those You Lead: Discretionary versus Non-Discretionary Effort

I've spent a lot of time thinking about ways to approach the idea of discretionary versus non-discretionary effort. Non-discretionary effort is the minimum standard of effort we expect employees to do in performing the duties of their job. To be more direct, we hire them to do a job, and their job is to do certain things, such as sell something, build something, fix something, etc. They fulfill the parameters of their job description to receive their agreed-upon remuneration. There are also minimum standards of performance. There may be certain consequences if they don't meet these standards, which could include warnings, disciplinary actions, or termination. On the other hand, if an employee's work exceeds the standards, they might receive recognition, bonuses, and/or promotions.

Discretionary effort, however, is effort that employees exert of their own free will. It falls into two categories:

1. External drivers, such as a chance to receive some reward (recognition, a bonus, or a promotion)

2. Internal drivers, such as fear, inspiration, or engagement

The first category is simply based on a hope to reap some additional benefit beyond the established remuneration. The second category is based on fear (e.g., a fear of not being seen as a team player or hard worker, which could lead to a lack of opportunities for promotions, wage increases, or recognition) or inspiration/engagement (e.g., related to the way employees feel about their current job and their impact on the organization). This second category is when employees want to do more for reasons other than money, job advancement, or recognition.

Over the past several years, I have often asked the following question during my leadership development programs with managers: Assuming money, benefits, and promotions are off the table, from the list below, what are the top four things that inspire or engage people at work?

1. Inspiring work
2. Involvement in the decisions that affect me
3. Non-monetary recognition for a job well done
4. Autonomy
5. Flexibility (work hours, start times, etc.)
6. Contributing to a better world or society
7. Freedom and time to think and create beyond my normal job requirements
8. Ability to drive change
9. Contributing to improving efficiency and productivity
10. Development and growth
11. Other

The ones that typically come out on top are:

1. Inspiring work
2. Involvement in the decisions that affect me
3. Freedom and time to think and create beyond my normal job requirements
4. Autonomy

Inspiring Work

If people believe they add value to the organization, if they understand how they contribute to the larger mission, there is a greater chance they will feel inspired by their work. Think about your own experiences. Have you ever felt really inspired while working on a project? Managers can assist employees with this by talking about the big picture and how they contribute to it.

They can also recognize people for the good work they do, whether it's part of their regular job or a special assignment.

Conversely, managers can also destroy inspiration by minimizing people's contributions, so a big part of being a leader is also about knowing how to avoid sabotaging your employees' capacity to be inspired by their work.

Involvement in the Decisions That Affect Me

Managers often tell me that involving people in decisions sometimes isn't possible because of time and money. Sometimes the decision is simply pushed down from the top. I'm prepared to resign myself to the fact that, yes, this does happen, but what happens during other times? Remember that some of the best ideas come from those who work on the job every day. If that's the case, why wouldn't you include people, especially when it affects their job?

Including people also helps promote buy-in from them. Even if including people in decisions isn't possible, make every effort to inform them about decisions as soon as possible to allow them time to absorb new information and talk about any changes that will affect them.

Freedom and Time to Think and Create Beyond My Normal Job Requirements

Some might suggest that just trying to get people to do their regular jobs is a challenge for most managers, so how can a manager find additional opportunities for employees to think and create beyond their normal job requirements? But as a brilliant and newly minted upwardly mobile manager, you might already have lots of ideas on how to do this. Here are a few more. Consider having an employee take part in a special committee that may be company-wide such as strategic planning, become a member of a committee for a senior recruitment or a brand focus group, or become a member of one of the volunteer community groups such as United Way or Junior Achievement. There may also be an opportunity for someone to work on a pet project. For example, in human resources, a compensation person might like to be part of a special project for designing a training program if they're currently taking a night school course at community college on employee training and development. There are usually lots of things happening outside your work area, and sometimes we think that people won't be interested or that people are too busy. You might be surprised by the response you get from them.

In addition, freeing people up to participate beyond their job can really inspire them to contribute more to the organization. I won't say it helps motivate them because I still believe that motivation is intrinsic. As such, the most a manager can hope to do is create an environment where people will be more likely to feel motivated.

The idea of working with a certain degree of freedom has always been one of my key driving factors. I realize that you don't want to have employees just roaming around doing whatever they want. Sure, there are certain rules they need to adhere to, but think about how you manage people. Do you stand over them and micromanage them? Do you give them the autonomy and trust to do what they were hired to do once you're confident they have the skills, knowledge, and experience?

On many occasions throughout my career, I've had a superior say to me, "I trust you, so go ahead and run with it. I need it by…." Was I successful? You bet. There was no way I was going to fail when I was presented with that much trust and autonomy.

Once you're sure people have the skills and knowledge necessary to complete a task and you have some degree of confidence in them, try giving them some autonomy. Just be careful not to set anyone up for failure. Regardless, mistakes are a form of learning. You need to weigh the risks associated with each task you assign.

So what does all of this tell us? Well, we can conclude that when money is taken out of the equation, there are certain things that act as catalysts in some people that might inspire them to use their discretionary effort and potentially go above and beyond what's expected of them. They do these things because they want to. They do them because it makes them feel good or because they feel good about the organization or the boss they work for. Maybe they do them because they feel some sort of ownership or loyalty to the organization. Regardless, discretionary effort is something that managers should nurture in employees. When employees use discretionary effort, they're not looking for additional pay, a bonus, or a promotion. If this is true, why wouldn't we want to create an environment where people feel inspired and engaged?

Establishing Boundaries

When you become a manager, you're no longer one of the boys or one of the girls. You're always on display, and you're treated differently. Your position at the helm helps you influence others, but this makes many new managers uncomfortable. To ease the transition to your new role, try establishing boundaries between your work life and personal life. These boundaries will help you establish credibility, trust, and respect—all of which are crucial if you want to positively influence others.

Rule 1: Be Aware of the Fishbowl Effect

Once you become a manager, you become a main point of interest for your employees. They will know when you arrive, when you leave, where you eat lunch, how long you talk on the phone, and who you spend your time with at work. If you think you have secrets from your employees, think again. They are incredibly observant and are often the first to identify substance abuse problems, office affairs, and changes in people's behaviour.

Rule 2: Set Guidelines for Staff Regarding What You Will and Won't Talk About with Them

This is especially critical if you attend social functions and participate in sports activities with staff. It's best to set the boundaries up front so there's no misunderstanding. "Look, although we're getting together to play volleyball, I don't want to talk about work. If you want to chat about something, come to my office tomorrow so we can discuss it." Simple statements like this send a clear message that you aren't going to engage in "shop talk" when you're in a social setting.

If people persist in trying to get you to comment on work situations, you may need to stop attending certain social functions (especially if alcohol is involved). One new supervisor I spoke with recently told me the strategy she uses during department social functions. She shows up for the first thirty minutes, mingles with everyone while having a cocktail, and then appropriately excuses herself and lets the festivities continue. By doing this, she makes an appearance at the event but leaves before alcohol (and perhaps good judgment) might affect the situation.

Rule 3: Don't Be the Drunkest One at the Party

This rule applies to many areas of your managerial role: trust, influence, and credibility. In the past, no one talked about how drunk the boss got at the office party, except in whispers behind closed doors. Today, the drunken boss episode will be an open discussion topic at the water cooler, during lunch, at the boardroom table, and on Facebook! Social media has opened businesses to greater public scrutiny. Managers now need to practice discretion to maintain their reputation and the reputation of their company.

This rule doesn't just apply to intoxication; it also applies to drunken behaviour. Don't be the loudest and most obnoxious know-it-all in the room. Overall, certain behaviours were more acceptable at office parties in the fifties and sixties but are no longer acceptable today. Most organizations are no longer impressed by the amount of liquor people can hold or how well they can dance on a table while wearing lampshade.

Establishing boundaries will have a positive effect on your managerial role. Communication is the key to establishing and maintaining clear and healthy boundaries. We've discussed how developing yourself and your employees will benefit you on your voyage toward success, but knowing your employees and acknowledging their differences will foster respectful and productive relationships.

Coaching and Mentoring: Do It, Get It

People sometimes get to the position of manager and believe they no longer need to learn anymore because they already have all the answers. As you can imagine, this is a dangerous place to be, but it's not uncommon.

Once you've been promoted to your first position in management, it becomes even more critical to look for assistance and support from those who have been successful in more senior positions. I cannot emphasize this enough. Having someone to call on when you need a sounding board, someone who can act as your unbiased confidant, can be invaluable to your long-term sanity. This could be a mentor or a coach. It shouldn't be your spouse, however, regardless of how much you trust them, as they're too close to you and therefore probably quite biased in your favour. Although this is wonderfully supportive, it's not in your best interest if you want unbiased advice or a reality check.

I have always had trusted associates to rely on in this role. Every few months, I would check in with them. I would sometimes also hire the services of a professional coach at my own personal expense, but this isn't absolutely necessary. The idea is to have a conversation about your career with someone who will be completely honest with you.

Coaches and mentors are different. In my view, a mentor is someone who has more often than not had experience in your area. Their perspective on how to proceed is often invaluable, and they can easily point out both the good and the bad. A coach, on the other hand, may or may not have experience in your particular area. Their expertise is more about asking the right questions and pushing the right buttons to get you thinking about things differently.

Here are some questions to consider before getting involved with a coach or a mentor.

1. Are you willing to accept critical advice and open to challenges to help you in your personal

growth and development?

2. Do you know someone who can provide you with a good perspective while keeping your best interests in mind? Will this person be honest and tough when the situation requires it?

3. Is there someone you don't know personally who you would like to be your mentor and/or coach? Are you willing to approach them?

Keep in mind that coaching and mentoring are cyclical. In other words, the more coaching and mentoring you receive, the more likely you will be asked to coach or mentor someone else one day.

Chapter 12

Captain's Log: Your Next Voyage

You've completed your captain's log from the last voyage and have started to put together a plan for your next voyage. Maybe everything went perfectly last time and you wouldn't change a thing. On the other hand, maybe you want to make several changes before you head out there again.

Certainly, from a leadership perspective, I don't believe you ever get things perfect. The people who report to you are unique, complex, and dynamic beings. They will continue to grow and change. As such, you will need to continue to grow and change as a leader.

You've learned many things from being out on the open water and being in command. Now start to think about the next trip and how you would like to approach it. The end of one trip is often the beginning of the next. Keep in mind that every trip won't be smooth sailing, nor will every trip be fraught with danger. Although we need to be prepared for the unknown, we shouldn't remain fearful of impending doom.

It's important for you to learn from every experience. As a leader, you will find that every day is a new experience. Try to be deliberate in your self-reflection and in thinking about everything that happens. In other words, ask yourself questions such as the following.

1. What happened today?
2. What was my involvement?
3. What could I have done better?
4. What could I have done differently?
5. What did I learn?

I recently had a very enlightening conversation with a colleague that reinforced the questions above. I was, to say the least, impressed with how many answers and suggestions he had to almost every question or concern I had regarding leadership challenges I was addressing in an organization similar to the one he had recently retired from. It shouldn't have come as a surprise to me because he had been the president of the organization for eighteen years and had accumulated a tremendous amount of experience at the most senior level.

He had many good answers and had experienced many of the same situations—in some cases, several times—so it was surprising to me when he said that he was still learning regardless of what he had already done. Sure, he had a lot of experience, but the formula is always changing because each challenge involves different people, different situations, different time frames, and different internal and/or external forces.

He said that the advantage of having experience is that you aren't starting at ground zero. Instead, you're adapting, experimenting, and challenging the things that worked in the past with new situations, so you're always learning and building your library. You should always be learning even if it's just to confirm that you did the right thing while changing and evolving as you go. As Muhammad Ali once said, "A man who views the world the same at fifty as he did at twenty has wasted thirty years of his life."

In this book, I may have presented a very different picture from what you experienced while studying at university or college. The information that matters isn't necessarily derived from theoretical rhetoric or quantitative research methodologies. In a sense, you will begin acquiring the most valuable information the day you arrive at your first management position. In fairness, some companies have been addressing these issues for many years. I hope this book will help you traverse the corporate minefield relatively unscathed by helping you apply some of the key concepts. If there's one thing you absolutely need to take from this book, it's the importance of relationships and how they affect influence.

Maybe you already have very good technical skills. Maybe you already manage your people satisfactorily. The question, however, becomes do you want to be good or do you want to be great? In his book *Good to Great*, Jim Collins states on the first page that "good is the enemy of great." So how do you become a great manager rather than a good manager?

Elsewhere in this book, I referred to a survey I conducted recently with some human resources professionals who excel in their area. I performed a theme analysis on the responses, and the number one finding from the participants was that new managers can greatly enhance their effectiveness and success by building or strengthening relationships with staff, as this increases the opportunities for positive influence. As I mentioned before, there is no leadership without influence.

This seems simple to me. If you look after your people and treat them with respect and honesty, there's a good chance they will look after your customers, which can easily contribute to profitability. I summarize this in an equation below.

The Success Equation

Make a quality product or provide a quality service that people want and get it to market, price it properly, and consistently improve it

$+$

Hire the right people and then engage them (set expectations, hold people accountable, recognize them, and be honest with them)

$=$

A ton of money!

The secret: Every once in a while, you actually have to talk with your employees!

I also discussed leadership with a colleague of mine, Cara Krezek, the director of co-op, career, and experiential education at Brock University. She started her career in management in the private sector. She shared this story with me.

When I started my management career, I was in my early twenties and working for a company that used their mission, vision, and values as their guiding compass for everything we did. From the time I started with Enterprise, it was ingrained in me that you take care of your people first, and they in turn will take care of our customers, and the growth and profits will follow.

So while at a young age, I had the responsibility of six staff and millions of dollars in operations and inventory. I also had a vision and guiding values to get behind. This taught me how to make decisions I could frame in a way that I knew I was making the right choice. This allowed me to empower my staff to make the decisions using the same guiding principles.

It is also a lesson that I have carried with me throughout my career. Give people the vision, mission, and values; live those values; and use them to bring people onboard and when you need to make an intentional break with an employee, when you have to make a tough decision or a choice between multiple factors.

The values are the "wall" that you can bounce things off and test things with, and they keep us moving in the same direction. Integrating these values into everything we do makes for a strong team and allows management to empower and engage employees to take control of the everyday decisions that align with organizational goals and objectives.

Many organizations talk about having a vision, a mission, and values. They often post them on big plaques in the reception area so customers and visitors can see them and perhaps be impressed by them when they arrive. The key is to make sure that all employees actually adhere to them, including (and most importantly) senior management. More often than not, they don't.

If the vision, mission, and values are followed and become ingrained in the organization, then employees can use them as guides for making decisions. Developing them and living by them is another way to support and guide your employees. It gives employees standards to live up to and be proud of. As Cara told me, it makes for a strong team and allows management to empower and engage employees.

Final Thoughts

Whatever happens as a result of your decision to pursue a management position and continue the climb upwards, life does go on. You will meet people who will support you, and you'll meet some who won't. Regardless, you can control only a certain amount of what will ultimately happen to you.

My sense is that if you get to the point where you believe you have arrived and you have everything figured out, you will actually be at the most vulnerable point in your professional life. We limit ourselves when we think we know everything and have all the answers. Throughout my career, which has been rewarding and often exciting, it has always been the people I have worked with that made things either great or lousy. Fortunately, the latter experiences have been few and far between and so require little mention. Over the years, although I would leave organizations, I would never really leave the people, and some of them have become lifelong friends. On the other hand, I also realize that some of the positive outcomes were a direct result of the management and leadership style I adopted early on.

I have thought about, researched, studied, and applied what I believe are solid leadership principles for most of my working life. I have worked with and for a variety of managers throughout that time, some good, some not so bad, some just downright lousy, and probably two that I would describe as great. I would also suggest that not only were they great managers; they were also great leaders. Fortunately, I worked for these great managers early in my career, and their influence has affected me this whole time. I have also had the opportunity to work for some good leaders, some early in their careers but where I saw the respect they had already earned from their employees. Remember, as I said, I haven't really met any bad leaders because I don't believe bad leadership exists. Bad leadership means no leadership.

It still amazes and baffles me that so many lousy, dishonest, and incompetent managers actually survive in organizations for as long as they do. In many cases, it's because their bosses often tolerate them, and this is often because these managers meet their quantifiable goals. It doesn't matter how they treat people. As long as they make their numbers, they're considered good leaders.

I think we are losing tolerance for this type of manager, as more employees are now coming forward with claims of harassment and bullying. I suspect that we will see more of this in the future as employees feel less inclined to accept poor or intimidating behaviour from their bosses. More organizations are becoming less sympathetic or supportive of these types of managers, in part because human rights and bullying cases can cost companies money and have a huge impact on reputation.

Yet, it seems so easy to be great. Here are some of the guiding principles I have used as my standard. I hope you will find them helpful.

1. *Be honest, be honest, be honest.* Nothing can replace this. Remember, trust is difficult to earn, easy to lose, and almost impossible to regain.

2. *Be supportive*. Talk to your people, understand them, work with them, and stand shoulder to shoulder with them when necessary.

3. *Hold people accountable and deal with substandard behaviour*. Have the honest conversation with them. Not everyone will work out, so deal with it and allow people who don't fit to move on.

4. *Tell people what's going on*. This is especially important when things affect people's jobs. Include them in decisions about their jobs where possible.

5. *Let people know when things are going well*. Look for people doing things right and recognize them for it.

6. *Manage your emotions and ego*. Remember that everybody in the organization contributes to the success of the organization.

Be proud of the work you do. Management isn't for everyone. Those who excel at management and leadership are a rare breed. Stay curious. The world will continue to change and evolve, and you will need to continue to tweak and expand your skills sets. Finally, forge ahead. Don't be discouraged by failure or lousy bosses. Tenacity and courage will win the day. Good luck on your next voyage.

Recommended Reading

1. *The Five Dysfunctions of a Team*, Patrick Lencioni
2. *Switch: How to Change Things When Change Is Hard*, Chip and Dan Heath
3. *The 7 Habits of Highly Successful People: Powerful Lessons in Personal Change*, Stephen Covey
4. *Crucial Conversations: Tools for Talking When Stakes Are High*, Kerry Patterson, Joseph Grenny, Ron McMillan, and Al Switzler
5. *Boundaries for Leaders: Results, Relationships, and Being Ridiculously in Charge*, Henry Cloud
6. *Forged in Crisis: The Power of Courageous Leadership in Turbulent Times*, Nancy Koehn
7. *What Millennials Want from Work: How to Maximize Engagement in Today's Workforce*, Jennifer J. Deal and Alec Levenson
8. *First, Break All the Rules: What the World's Greatest Managers Do Differently*, Marcus Buckingham and Curt Coffman
9. *The Power of Habit: Why We Do What We Do in Life and Business*, Charles Duhigg

Acknowledgements

This book is a product of a lifetime of observing and engaging in management and leadership. It's a book about my experiences in observing many leaders and followers. Their stories and my interactions and relationships with them brought me to this point in my life. There are many stories, good and bad, that I wasn't able to tell in this book, but they certainly played a role in informing me in my research and practical applications.

The stories are one thing, but putting the words together in a compelling way is an art in itself and one that has eluded me thus far. I jumbled and shuffled many words together into a manuscript, but it was my editor, Dan Varrette, who was able to craft them into a readable and hopefully informative book. Thank you, Dan!

Many other people have acted as guideposts along the way. My friend and colleague Dr. Barry Wright was the first to suggest I focus my writing on the new frontline manager because of the importance of this position and the lack of materials available. Ms. Draj Fozard, what can I say? You opened a magical door for me. I would also like to thank my colleagues and friends Cara Krezek and Neil Culp, who advised me on surveys, LinkedIn blogs and videos, and general advice. I would also like to thank Bob Ruttan and Bob Stewart, two extraordinary leaders who set me on the path.

To the fabulous Caren, my partner in crime. Your

advice and critical analysis have been priceless. To my dad, who reminded me during my early sports years to not read my own press clippings, to keep my head up, and, if in doubt, to shoot the puck at the net. To my grandfather, a tough, old French Canadian who started work at thirteen years old at a logging camp in Northern Ontario and who served in the First and Second World Wars. You reminded me on many occasions that I could accomplish anything.

To the generations who came before me, including my great-grandmother and great-great-grandmother, who survived, at least physically, the residential schools in Ontario. Also to the generations of the future, including my children and grandchildren, who are my purpose and passion to push on.

Finally, to Mike O'Connor at Insomniac Press. Thanks for taking a chance on a proud first-time Canadian author.

CPSIA information can be obtained
at www.ICGtesting.com
Printed in the USA
LVHW010303071218
599536LV00002B/2